Public Diplomacy and Civil Society Organisations

This book explores the roles of civil society organisations (CSOs) when engaging in public diplomacy activities and their impact on community development and change. It provides up-to-date analysis of the challenges and constraints facing CSOs involved in diplomatic missions and working with foreign donors.

Bringing together case studies from Cameroon, Egypt, Poland, Palestine, Lebanon and Libya, this edited collection reflects on how external calls for proposals in the fields of women's empowerment, community development, education, training, exchange programmes, democracy, human rights and peacebuilding influence the way civil society organisations contribute, deliver, intervene and position themselves in various societies. It explores the lessons learnt by various CSOs in identifying societal problems, understanding grassroots demands, prioritising development agendas and campaigning for peacebuilding. Grounded in a firm theoretical framework and based on up-to-date empirical research, the book reflects on the leadership shown by civil society organisations in development, politics and business and their impact on community development initiatives and local change process.

This book will be an important resource for researchers, policymakers, donors, NGO practitioners and the beneficiaries themselves, within the areas of international development, peacebuilding, civil society, politics and international relations.

Ibrahim Natil has published many works, including seven books, taught at different academic institutions and worked for many civil society and international organisations. He is an Associate Professor of International Relations and Diplomacy and Assistant Dean for Programs at Joaan Bin Jasim Academy for Defence Studies and a Research Fellow at the Institute of International Conflict Resolution and Re-construction (IICRR) at Dublin City University, Ireland. He is also the Co-convenor of NGOs in Development Study Group, DSA-UK, and the founder of Society Voice Foundation and winner of the Robert Chamber Best Overall Paper, selected by DSA Ireland (2017). He has invited a guest and visiting lecturer to a number of universities and has acted as an external examiner at a number of well-known universities such as Glasgow Caledonian (2021), Durham University (2020) and Bradford University (2018/2021). He also managed more than 60 community projects in the field of human rights, community peacebuilding and women and youth empowerment since 1997.

Routledge Explorations in Development Studies

This Development Studies series features innovative and original research at the regional and global scale. It promotes interdisciplinary scholarly works drawing on a wide spectrum of subject areas, in particular politics, health, economics, rural and urban studies, sociology, environment, anthropology, and conflict studies.

Topics of particular interest are globalization; emerging powers; children and youth; cities; education; media and communication; technology development; and climate change.

In terms of theory and method, rather than basing itself on any orthodoxy, the series draws broadly on the tool kit of the social sciences in general, emphasizing comparison, the analysis of the structure and processes, and the application of qualitative and quantitative methods.

Sweden's Research Aid Policy
The Role of Science in Development
Veronica Brodén Gyberg

Gender, Digitization, and Resilience in International Development
Failing Forward
Julia Bello-Bravo, John William Medendorp, Anne Namatsi Lutomia, and Barry Robert Pittendrigh

Multinationals, Poverty Alleviation and UK Aid
The Complex Quest for Mutually Beneficial Outcomes
Jo-Anna Russon

Public Diplomacy and Civil Society Organisations
Edited by Ibrahim Natil

For more information about this series, please visit: www.routledge.com/Routledge-Explorations-in-Development-Studies/book-series/REDS

Public Diplomacy and Civil Society Organisations

Edited by Ibrahim Natil

LONDON AND NEW YORK

First published 2024
by Routledge
4 Park Square, Milton Park, Abingdon, Oxon OX14 4RN

and by Routledge
605 Third Avenue, New York, NY 10158

Routledge is an imprint of the Taylor & Francis Group, an informa business

© 2024 selection and editorial matter, Ibrahim Natil; individual chapters, the contributors

The right of Ibrahim Natil to be identified as the author of the editorial material, and of the authors for their individual chapters, has been asserted in accordance with sections 77 and 78 of the Copyright, Designs and Patents Act 1988.

All rights reserved. No part of this book may be reprinted or reproduced or utilised in any form or by any electronic, mechanical, or other means, now known or hereafter invented, including photocopying and recording, or in any information storage or retrieval system, without permission in writing from the publishers.

Trademark notice: Product or corporate names may be trademarks or registered trademarks, and are used only for identification and explanation without intent to infringe.

British Library Cataloguing-in-Publication Data
A catalogue record for this book is available from the British Library

Library of Congress Cataloguing-in-Publication Data
Names: Natil, Ibrahim, editor.
Title: Public diplomacy and civil society organisations / edited by Ibrahim Natil.
Description: Abingdon, Oxon ; New York, NY : Routledge, 2024. | Series: Routledge explorations in development studies | Includes bibliographical references and index.
Identifiers: LCCN 2023027476 (print) | LCCN 2023027477 (ebook) | ISBN 9781032578897 (hardback) | ISBN 9781032578903 (paperback) | ISBN 9781003441465 (ebook)
Subjects: LCSH: Non-governmental organizations. | Civil society. | Diplomacy.
Classification: LCC JZ4841 .P83 2024 (print) | LCC JZ4841 (ebook) | DDC 361.7/7--dc23/eng/20230824
LC record available at https://lccn.loc.gov/2023027476
LC ebook record available at https://lccn.loc.gov/2023027477

ISBN: 978-1-032-57889-7 (hbk)
ISBN: 978-1-032-57890-3 (pbk)
ISBN: 978-1-003-44146-5 (ebk)

DOI: 10.4324/9781003441465

Typeset in Times New Roman
by MPS Limited, Dehradun

Contents

List of Contributors	*vii*

1 Introducing public diplomacy in civil society
organisations   1
IBRAHIM NATIL

2 Exploring new concepts and practices in civil
society organisations' public diplomacy   9
IBRAHIM NATIL

3 Historical review of public diplomacy: Milestones
for civic engagement and business   19
MOHAMMAD AL-MAZAWDAH

4 Public diplomacy and civil society penetration:
The new 'scramble for Africa'   29
NGUH NWEI ASANGA FON

5 Being at the forefront: Polish CSOs' contribution
to public diplomacy and development cooperation
efforts   41
GALIA CHIMIAK AND KATARZYNA ZALAS-KAMIŃSKA

6 Barriers to CSOs' public diplomacy: Failure of
multilateral intervention, conflict, violence and
militarism   55
IBRAHIM NATIL

vi *Contents*

7 Civil society organisations' public diplomacy and
   youth political participation in Egypt   74
   AHMED EL ASSAL AND AMR MARZOUK

8 Challenges to civil society organisations' public
   diplomacy: Militarism, restrictions and violence
   in Libya and Lebanon   93
   IBRAHIM NATIL

9 Concluding thoughts: New directions for civil
   society organisations' public diplomacy   106
   IBRAHIM NATIL

   Index   *113*

Contributors

Mohammad Al-Mazawdah is an Associate Professor of Islamic History and Islamic Civilization at Qatar University. Dr Al-Mazawdah holds a PhD in history Andalusian from the University of Granada, Spain (2014), and worked as an Associate Professor at Yarmouk University, the Dean of Student Affairs at Yarmouk University in Jordan (2020–2021) and the Head of the History Department at Yarmouk University (2018–2020).

Nguh Nwei Asanga Fon is a PhD candidate in International Relations at Eastern Mediterranean University, North Cyprus. His research interests include governance, development studies, foreign policy, conflict resolution and African politics. He has several publications in peer-reviewed journals and international conference presentations. He is a research fellow with the International Governance Institute (IGI) Cameroon and a member of the International Association for Political Science Students (IAPSS). Professionally, he has a rich experience as a civil society leader in Cameroon having served as an Executive Director of Community Awareness and Development Association Cameroon (CADAC) for 10 years (2013–2022).

Galia Chimiak is an Associate Professor at the Civil Society Department with the Institute of Philosophy and Sociology, Polish Academy of Sciences in Warsaw. Her main research interests are in CSOs, their human resources, development cooperation and global education. She is a co-editor-in-chief of *VOLUNTAS: International Journal of Voluntary and Nonprofit Organization* (published by Springer Nature) and a former Convenor of the Civil Society Study Group with Development Studies Association Ireland.

Ahmed El Assal is a PhD researcher and Marie Skłodowska–Curie research fellow at the International Institute of Social Studies (ISS), Erasmus University Rotterdam. He holds an MA in Governance, Development and Public Policy from the Institute of Development

viii *Contributors*

Studies (IDS), University of Sussex. He has more than a decade of experience in the international development sector, with a particular focus on intersections of governance, human rights and economic justice issues. His research focuses on civil society, foreign aid, accountability and public service delivery.

Amr Marzouk is a Phd researcher at the Department of Law, Society and Crime at Erasmus University Rotterdam and he holds an MSc in Criminology from Durham University. His research work focuses on issues related to criminology, social movements and cyber politics.

Katarzyna Zalas-Kamińska is an Assistant Professor at the Institute of Political Studies at the University of Wrocław. Her research interests are public diplomacy and development cooperation. She cooperates with Polish NGOs (including *Grupa Zagranica*, a platform of organizations involved in development cooperation, democracy support and global education), as well as with the Ministry of Foreign Affairs in Poland (as a member of the Development Cooperation Policy Council 2020–2024).

1 Introducing public diplomacy in civil society organisations

Ibrahim Natil

Introduction

With their diverse range of organisations, objectives and activities that target local, national and global issues, civil society organisations (CSOs) play an increasingly important role in the political, economic and social dynamics that shape daily lives across the world today. The CSO sector is a wide-ranging field characterised by dynamic relationships with local and international actors. This volume explores the roles of CSOs when engaging in public diplomacy activities and their impact on community development and change. CSOs' engagement is considered a significant agent for changing and developing societies in response to donors' agendas and shifts in a digital world. They have a considerable impact and influence on social and community development. This volume is keen to publish research that provides up-to-date analysis of challenges and constraints facing CSOs' public diplomacy actions, which are essential tools to achieve their visions and missions in the field of development and change.

The chapters analyse the extent to which CSOs have employed social media platforms to facilitate the operations of their organisations in responding to donors' conditions and their grassroots demands and needs. The use of technology for public diplomacy tools by CSOs could potentially affect the marginalisation of groups without access to the internet, which risks the domination of social change and community development requirements and conditions. This domination could strengthen CSOs' engagement and their leaders' power over grassroots groups, and target groups would benefit more from donor-funded projects in the fields of community development and social change. These perceptions of CSOs and their grassroots movements of public diplomacy campaigns should not contradict the CSOs' missions in achieving their objective to promote human security and community development processes at different levels.

The volume explores the lessons learnt by various CSOs and their target groups, despite cultural differences and social context constraints, identifying societal problems, understanding grassroots demands,

DOI: 10.4324/9781003441465-1

2 Ibrahim Natil

prioritising development agendas and campaigning for peacebuilding. It also aims to explore how CSOs engage in public diplomacy campaigns in various contexts, which will be important for different target audiences, including scientists, researchers, national-level policymakers, donors, NGO staff and the beneficiaries themselves. Each of these groups has different priorities, needs and agendas. These processes often undermine and block CSOs' scope of work, engagement and contribution to development and change processes. In many contexts, however, it is largely about the ways CSOs respond, react and prioritise civil society actions and donors' agendas. CSOs face high levels of societal demands at the local level while also engaging in and responding to international communications with various actors, including donors and human rights activists. There are different definitions for CSOs; however, Asian development bank defines CSOs as:

> Civil society organizations (CSOs) are non-state actors whose aims are neither to generate profits nor to seek governing power. CSOs unite people to advance shared goals and interests. They have a presence in public life, expressing the interests and values of their members or others, and are based on ethical, cultural, scientific, religious, or philanthropic considerations. CSOs include nongovernment organizations (NGOs), professional associations, foundations, independent research institutes, community-based organizations (CBOs), faith-based organizations, people's organizations, social movements, and labor unions.
>
> (Asian development bank, 2009)

To explore new examples of CSOs' public diplomacy, this volume brings some case studies from various places around the world (the Cameron, Poland, Lebanon, Palestine, Libya and Egypt) to highlight the challenges and opportunities of engaging CSOs with diplomatic missions and foreign donors. To what extent do CSOs engage in public diplomacy activities? What is the relationship between diplomatic missions' "public diplomacy" and CSOs? What are the distinctive dimensions of development and public diplomacy, if any? Which innovative/alternative forms might CSOs take in terms of public diplomacy campaigns? The chapters in this book seek to answer these and other questions. This volume also focuses on the relationship and engagement between certain civil society actors/organisations and diplomatic missions, embassies and consulates in relation to various activities, including financial donations, exchange programmes, training, meetings, field visits, scholarship, etc. To what extent and how did diplomatic missions promote equality and justice within the CSO sector through public diplomacy in the context of the global pandemic? Is there a negative or a positive side to CSOs'

Introducing public diplomacy in civil society organisations   3

engagement with diplomatic missions' public diplomacy campaigns, and what can be learnt from them? The chapters provide overviews of some diplomatic missions/international donors' interests and values in supporting civil society projects. They examine the impact of CSOs on local politics, power and social and political life and explore the lessons learnt from certain CSOs supported by diplomatic missions/international donors despite divisions, violence, social conservatism, lack of opportunities and the role of various political systems in this regard (Natil et al., 2020). Andrew Cooper (2015) argues about the importance of diplomacy along with its attendant capacity—albeit with many constraints and frustration for adaptation. The chapters consider case studies of CSOs' engagement with foreign missions, embassies, consulates, actors/donors and foreign aid organisations. The volume brings together contributions from different parts of the world to promote cooperation between societies and communities across the globe so as to advance our understanding of CSOs from different perspectives and how they can contribute to making societies more just and equal. It examines why CSOs have considered the themes or strategies of public diplomacy in their operations while applying for foreign grants despite the challenges of civic engagement, as there are a number of CSOs and human rights activists who are fighting for the decolonisation of foreign aid or calling for CSOs to stop relying on external (foreign) funding. These practical issues of public diplomacy including the power and powerless of state- and non-state actors to contribute significant changes also discussed by Paul Webster et al. (2023). It asks, for example, to what extent has the concept of decolonising foreign aid affected public diplomacy activities run by diplomatic missions and CSOs? What strategies, processes and material conditions encourage development in CSOs' engagement in public diplomacy? What are the distinctive challenges faced by CSOs? Some human rights activists believe that foreign aid is not sustainable or does not help development processes; however, defenders of foreign aid believe that the recipient CSOs facilitating training, scholarships and exchange programmes assist individuals to improve their skills, knowledge and lifestyle in the long term.

The cases also highlight the role of foreign diplomatic missions and their public diplomacy activities and engagement with CSOs through, in Holm's words (2020a), "street-level diplomacy" and "small grants". Diplomatic missions have good relationships with CSOs implementing local development projects in different fields, such as human rights, women's empowerment, peacebuilding, justice and equality, etc. However, security circumstances and/or local challenges, such as COVID-19, affect the relations between the funders (diplomatic missions) and aid recipients owing to changes in the countries' priorities, staff movements, travel

4 *Ibrahim Natil*

restrictions and political shifts at home and abroad. The volume also discusses how CSOs and diplomatic missions/donors have employed digital technology tools to replace traditional channels of communication, such as in-person meetings and field visits.

Nancy Snow and Nicholas J. Cull (2020) discuss the significance of digital and corporate public diplomacy. However, foreign aid remains a crucial issue for CSOs' operations in the field of development and remains a tool of soft power for diplomatic missions' public diplomacy activities (Alexander, 2018), as discussed. Shifts in financial support and/ or priorities decide on the nature of the relationship between the two sides. Financial support, for example, determines the future of the relationship and engagement, which affects the sustainability of CSOs' contributions to local development projects regardless of their level of public diplomacy engagement during the cycle of funding. CSOs' implementation of local projects in partnership with international NGOs, however, has a different engagement process to that with foreign diplomatic missions (Holm, 2020b).

This volume will be highly influential as it contains in-depth understanding and evidence of particular CSOs' responses to calls for proposals in the fields of women's empowerment, community development, education, training, exchange programmes, democracy, human rights and peacebuilding, prioritised or and identified by donors' and diplomatic missions' agendas. Presenting up-to-date empirical research helps to understand the significance of CSOs' engagement with and contribution to grassroots actions in the field of community development and change. The book also aims at improving our understanding of how these issues/themes influence the way CSOs contribute, deliver, intervene and position themselves in various societies. Particular emphasis is placed upon the challenges faced by CSOs from locations that are linked not only to conflict constraints but also to technical and policy constraints that are crucial markers of development and change. Remarkably, although considerable research has highlighted the weaknesses and limitations of CSOs' influence and power, rather less attention has been paid to the legislation and policies that result in the exceptional circumstances and dynamics characterising some societies in which CSOs find themselves.

Therefore, the volume offers new insights into how CSOs in such countries are shaped by and react to shifts, policies, conflicts, constraints and challenges while running public diplomacy campaigns. It also provides up-to-date analysis of CSOs' development challenges, opportunities and lessons learnt from The Cameroon, Poland, Palestine, Egypt, Libya and Lebanon. It is innovative and different as it mainly stems from the experiences and fieldwork of young contributors from these regions, enriching the debate on various developments with new insights and fresh perspectives, particularly from the Global South. The chapters

Introducing public diplomacy in civil society organisations 5

are structured around the theme of the demonstrated CSOs' public diplomacy in development action and practice, and they are further subdivided into "proactive and active" public diplomacy and "grants diplomacy" to make the edited volume more coherent. It discusses a number of definition in reference to local culture, social background and political contexts. It is divided into nine chapters, which are grouped together by the themes: *public diplomacy and civil society organisations.* Natil's (2022) theoretical chapter in this volume is specifically for the purpose of providing this balance.

The other chapters are empirical, but each chapter also discusses the theories and methodologies relevant to its country case study. Therefore, the balance between theoretical/methodological and empirical discussions is ensured. For example, Natil's chapters introduce explorations of CSOs' public diplomacy engagement, practices and influences in which they work and shed light on their challenges in contemporary societies. It includes the background, framework, scope and questions of volume and methods. It focuses on the theme of CSOs' responses to societal demands, donors' demands, shifts and changes and development challenges and opportunities by examining specific case studies, aiming at improving our understanding of the challenges facing CSOs' public diplomacy activities in various societies. Natil's introductory chapter and conclusion provide a sound theoretical and structural guidance for the reader in which to place each individual case study chapter. The introduction and conclusion also place the scope of the book into the wider framework of the academic discussion about the topic, so there is clear reference to related materials and themes within which this volume is situated. This assists to explore the effects of CSOs' engagement in responding to donors and/or diplomatic missions' public diplomacy and if CSOs interpret the concept of public diplomacy from the liberal perspective of international relations, as discussed by Broś (2017).

The chapters will tackle a number of challenges facing CSOs' effectiveness, the efficiency of their public diplomacy activities and their impact on change and community development processes. For example, CSOs now employ online and social media platforms to challenge restrictions imposed on activists' freedom of movement and lack of resources, including providing finance for their target groups and donors. The spread of diseases, wars and a lack of safety have increased pressure on CSOs to find alternative means to achieve their objectives. Natil talks about CSOs' public diplomacy challenges and opportunities and provides some up-to-date data on the countries mentioned in the book from relevant research groups and international organisations about the status of the impact of CSOs' public diplomacy. How do the local cultural and social contexts and backgrounds affect CSOs' public diplomacy tools, activities and engagement in local politics? To what

6   *Ibrahim Natil*

extent have CSOs' public diplomacy activities contributed to change and development processes despite social, political and health shifts?

This chapter explores the extent to which CSOs leaders employ the tools of public diplomacy activities to help grassroots groups to decide on future changes to their society despite conflicts, a lack of policies, restrictive political environments and the complexity of their sociocultural and economic context (Natil et al., 2020). It also discusses the development process of public diplomacy concepts and practices by giving the reader an idea about the contemporary history of these definitions. In Chapter 3, *Mohammad Al-Mazawdah* presents a historical introduction to public diplomacy in Granada, the Hafsid state and the Banu Marin based on deep readings and analysis of the Aragonese archives. *Al-Mazawdah's* work introduces development of "public diplomacy" and its relationship with civil society from a historical perspective when the consuls took care of the community of citizens at Aragonese, which was important to the development of the care of their commercial and business interests.

Contemporarily, the questions of CSOs' engagement in public diplomacy in Africa are discussed by Nguh Nwei Asanga Fon in chapter (4). Fon's analysis presents a critical overview of competition among great powers and how CSOs' engaging in their activities. However, Galia Chimiak and Katarzyna Zalas-Kamińska in chapter (5) discuss CSOs' engagement in public policy, development cooperation and democratisation from a Polish perspective as well. Both authors focus on the distinctive characteristics of Polish CSOs and their cooperation with national and international stakeholders, including their work with Ukrainian partners prior to the ongoing war in Ukraine. The paper will seek to elucidate Polish CSOs' potential to impact political and social life at home as well as abroad, as well as the most distinctive issues they face with regard to enhancing their own social power at home and impact on developments abroad.

The chapter enriches the current debate on CSOs' public diplomacy campaigns by extending it to COVID-19 and violence and militarism in the Palestine chapter (6). It provides the reader with empirically based and up-to-date but scientifically grounded analyses of civil society developments in Palestine. It will appeal not only to an academic audience but also to international agencies, policymakers and practitioners active in the specified regions. *Natil's* chapter also assesses the contexts and engages policymakers with rigorous empirical research in a systematic way. CSOs use public diplomacy tools, practices, campaigns and strategies to overcome both the internal and external challenges they face.

This book aims to bring about a heightened awareness of these challenges as well as highlight the potential for greater policy engagement for CSO leaders and for them to make great contributions to policy

Introducing public diplomacy in civil society organisations 7

changes, e.g., eradicating poverty. However, attempts to change policies are reflected by *Ahmed El Assal* and Amr Marzouk in chapter (7) which examines youth leaders' engagement in public diplomacy and political participation activities. The authors study how political shifts affected donor-driven civil society efforts in the realm of youth political participation programmes and how semi-authoritarian regimes reshape youth participation initiatives to support their rhetoric and gain regime loyalty. Despite donor funding for youth programmes in Egypt, CSOs could not advance them and consolidate their existence as influential actors in supporting youth participation, mainly due to restrictions imposed on CSOs. Olsson (2013) discusses public diplomacy as a crisis communication tool when new demands impose on governments to engage with publics on a transnational level.

Natil's chapter (8) studies civil society public diplomacy in Libya and Lebanon and the impact of shifts, challenges and responses to militarism, restrictions and violence. It investigates important questions, including: to what extent have violence, militarism and COVID-19 challenged CSOs' scope of work, operations and missions in Libya and Lebanon? What are the pros and cons of COVID-19's impact on CSOs' shifts and challenges? The chapter studies these challenges and how CSOs have coped with these shifts, and it also examines at least two different CSOs from each country to identify the differences among the cultural contexts, political environments and social dynamics to understand these shifts and challenges. For example, societies in Libya and Lebanon have been enduring very severe circumstances owing to economic decline, the absence of reconciliation, violence/militarism and divisions, which have already created barriers to the effectiveness of CSOs in the field of civic engagement and local peacebuilding as (Natil, 2021) argues.

Most of the contributions included in the edited volume are written by scholars from various locations. The book thus enriches the current debate on the present and, especially, civil society in public diplomacy and development. The edited volume provides the reader with empirically based, up-to-date but still scientifically grounded analyses of civil society developments in countries (The Cameroon, Poland, Lebanon, Palestine, Libya and Egypt) that can be appealing not only to an academic audience but also to international agencies, policymakers and practitioners active in the region.

References

Alexander, C. (2018) The Soft Power of Development: Aid and Assistance as Public Diplomacy Activities. In: Servaes, J. (Ed.), *Handbook of Communication for Development and Social Change*. Springer. Singapore.

8 *Ibrahim Natil*

Asian Development Bank. (2009) *CSO Sourcebook: A Staff Guide to Cooperation with Civil Society Organizations*. Mandaluyong City, Phil.

Broś, N. (2017) Public diplomacy and cooperation with non-governmental organizations in the liberal perspective of international relations. *Journal of Education Culture and Society*, no 1, 2017.

Cooper, A. (2015) *The Oxford Handbook of Modern Diplomacy*. Oxford University Press. Oxford.

Holm, N. (2020a) Street-level diplomacy? Administrator reflections on small grant schemes as a public diplomacy tool. *Diplomacy & Statecraft*, *31*(3), 557–578. 10.1080/09592296.2020.1782678

Holm, N. (2020b) Making the cut: exploring application evaluation and programme accessibility in embassy-based small grant schemes. *Forum for Development Studies*, *47*(2), 327–350. 10.1080/08039410.2020.1739123

Natil, I., Malila, V., and Sai, Y. (Eds.). (2020) *Barriers to Effective Civil Society Organisations: Political, Social and Financial Shifts*. Routledge.

Natil, I. (2021) Introducing Challenges to Youth Civic Engagement and Local Peacebuilding. In: *Youth Civic Engagement and Local Peacebuilding in the Middle East and North Africa* (pp. 1–12). Routledge.

Natil, I. (2022) *New Leadership of Civil Society Organisations: Community Development and Engagement*. Routledge, Taylor and Francis Group. London and New York.

Olsson, E. (2013) Public diplomacy as a crisis communication tool. *Journal of International Communication*, *19*(2), 219–234, 10.1080/13216597.2013.838906

Snow, N., and Cull, N. J. (2020) *Routledge Handbook of Public Diplomacy*. Routledge.

Webster, P., Sanchez, J., and Weisbrode, K. (2023) *The Palgrave Handbook of Diplomatic Reform and Innovation*. The Palgrave.

2 Exploring new concepts and practices in civil society organisations' public diplomacy

Ibrahim Natil

Introduction

Public diplomacy can be distinguished from the old style or traditional engagement of diplomacy, and it is a source of soft power for countries abroad. It comprises efforts exerted by diplomats abroad to achieve the goals of their country abroad, brand and promote its image, and increase its influence or "soft power" (Song & Fanoulis, 2023). It is a form of open dialogue between diplomats and citizens. Diplomats can engage with citizens worldwide on multiple issues via various tools, including social media networks (Proedrou & Frangonikolopoulos, 2012). It is a component of foreign affairs undertaken abroad by engaging with global publics or citizens from a third country and brands the country's identity in the international arena. Public diplomacy efforts include engaging with local languages, updating websites, providing information, exchanging ideas and information about culture, trade and education, attending local events and inviting locals from civil society to celebrate a "national day" organised by a diplomatic mission (Song & Fanoulis, 2023).

The term "public diplomacy" has been used and known since the mid-1960s, when international actors began to understand, engage with and influence foreign audiences and global opinions (Pamment, 2014). The American diplomat Edward Gullion was among the first to coin the term "public diplomacy" when the United States launched a public relations war on the Soviet Union during the cold war (Helmers, 2016). Furthermore, Margot Wallström (2008) was among the first European Union politicians to use the term "public diplomacy". However, public diplomacy has been part of the global scene for much longer. In Chapter 3 of the present volume, Mohammad Al-Mazawdah conducts a historical review of public diplomacy in Granada, considering how diplomats engaged in business with local communities abroad and worked to protect domestic interests in the fields of business and trade.

DOI: 10.4324/9781003441465-2

10   *Ibrahim Natil*

However, the term is defined differently from one country to another. For example, the European Union defines it as:

> Public diplomacy deals with the influence of public attitudes. It seeks to promote EU interests by understanding, informing and influencing. It means clearly explaining the EU's goals, policies and activities and fostering understanding of these goals through dialogue with individual citizens, groups, institutions and the media.
>
> (European Commission, 2007, p. 12)

Many scholars of international relations, history and diplomacy have distinguished "public diplomacy" from "cultural diplomacy" and "soft power" to emphasise the significance of diplomats' work and interactions with foreign audiences abroad (Lamal & Gelder, 2021). Others have argued that public diplomacy is a two-way communication channel to promote dialogue and cooperation instead of competition by engaging with public figures, politicians, community leaders, non-governmental organisations (NGOs) and business people (Al-Tamimi et al., 2023, p. 25). According to Zielińska (2016), public diplomacy is a combination of information management, strategic communication and relationship building. However, listening, advocacy, cultural diplomacy, exchange diplomacy and international broadcasting are also key elements of public diplomacy (Cull, 2008). Ultimately, public diplomacy is a tool to promote a foreign country's global image by engaging with local community figures, various representatives and civil society organisations (CSOs) at different levels.

CSOs are non-state actors that play a crucial role in raising human rights issues, including women's empowerment, strengthening good governance and engaging in peacebuilding actions. Sport for development and peace is a priority for some CSOs and their engagement with international actors, and the role of grassroots sport in public diplomacy is discussed by Garamvölgyi et al. (2022). The Representative Office of Norway to the Palestinian Authority, for example, facilitates the participation of local grassroots football teams from the Gaza Strip at the Norway Cup (an annual youth football tournament). CSOs are primary stakeholders and actors in achieving the United Nations' Sustainable Development Goals (SDGs) in cooperation with various governments that employ "development diplomacy" as a part of their public diplomacy programme to achieve foreign policy goals and strategies (Zielińska, 2016).

Asdourian (2022) has previously discussed the concept of civil society diplomacy by characterising collective and connective actions for a shared cause; however, Broś (2017) considers the concept of public diplomacy from the liberal perspective of international relations. These

Exploring new concepts and practices 11

issues are the soft power for CSOs' missions, values, principles, philosophy, scope of work and deliveries (Natil, 2022, pp. 1–6).

In short, it raises and addresses the following questions: to what extent are CSOs' target groups cognisant and aware of public diplomacy strategies and objectives? How do grassroots groups engage in or react to public campaigns, for example, CSOs' social media activities? Are the perceptions of CSOs' leaders in line with their grassroots and/or target groups? What are the motivations of grassroots and target groups in contributing to CSOs' public diplomacy campaigns? Are there differences between the CSOs' leaders and the target groups who benefit from donor-funded projects?

This chapter assists the reader with understanding CSOs' tools and strategies of engagement. Holm (2020a) has previously looked at "small grant schemes" as a public diplomacy tool. Small aid and assistance grants are considered public diplomacy activities and accumulated soft power from international donors' perspectives, as Alexander says:

> Foreign aid and development assistance fit well within the remit of public diplomacy and soft power because it seeks to improve the attractiveness of the source within the minds of target domestic and international audiences, such is its positive propagation under prevailing ideology.
>
> (Alexander, 2018)

Is CSOs' engagement with their local communities and foreign donors considered a new form of "public diplomacy"? Is it a new concept of "active public diplomacy" or "proactive public diplomacy"? CSOs always have a local network of partners that are easily accessible to engage with, and donors can also benefit from them by promoting their image or "soft power" values by awarding a few small grants in the fields of development. CSOs are much faster and more efficient actors to engage with and may influence their societies at different levels; as Snow (2008) argues, CSOs can also readily access and communicate values to their communities.

Proactive public diplomacy

As Bherer et al. (2016) discuss, CSOs' engagement in a "public diplomacy" process is associated with top-down mechanism practices that allow CSO activists and leaders to engage with and contribute to the public sector. The diplomatic missions, however, set the agenda for the local CSOs when they call for proposals or applications for funding. These calls reflect the diplomatic mission's home country's core issues and interests in the host country. Subsequently, local CSOs compete over

12 *Ibrahim Natil*

access to minimal funding via foreign aid from the diplomatic mission or embassy schemes (Holm, 2020b).

CSOs' public engagement activities are keenly interested in donors' values and objectives set out in the call for applications, such as empowering human rights and raising awareness of the gender issue. As Fanoulis and Revelas (2023) argue, public diplomacy entails awareness raising, information dissemination and lobbying. CSOs benefit from the small grant scheme; however, the level of public relations or indirect public diplomacy campaigns they conduct for the local embassy or diplomatic mission exceeds the value of funding. In other words, the donors gain far more benefits than the CSOs, which promote the image of the donors.

CSOs' responses to a call for proposals or applications for funding launched by a diplomatic mission comprise local initiatives to assist, develop and/or empower targeted grassroots capacities, skills, knowledge, awareness and engagement in various fields of human rights, women empowerment, peacebuilding, food security, relief issues, sport, etc. CSOs respond to specific values or themes, such as women's empowerment, by publicising donors' supported activities, as discussed by Holm (2020a). CSOs' justification for engaging with a call from a foreign diplomatic mission is to satisfy the demands and needs of local communities in dire economic and financial circumstances. CSOs' leaders believe that CSOs' responses are in accordance with the national law of the nation within which they operate and are binding to international agreements (Natil, 2022, pp. 1–6).

The Society Voice Foundation (SVF) is a Gaza Strip-based CSO funded by a number of international organisations that sought funding for a project entitled "Empowerment of Women's Active Participation, Public Engagement and Gender Equality by Implementing Capacity Building and Advocacy Activities in the Gaza Strip". Accordingly, the SVF approached the Canada Fund for Local Initiatives (CFLI), a small grant scheme run by Canada's representative office in the Palestinian Authority. The funding application submitted to the CFLI included a specific section for an advocacy plan to promote communications to raise awareness about the project using traditional and social media. An SVF representative said in an interview:

> The SVF would design a banner that included the logo of Canada's representative office, and its financial support would be acknowledged and visible. The SVF would tweet about the project at least twice per week, and we would tag Canada's representative office. There would be monthly blog posts about the project's progression/ results and Canada's contribution throughout the project's timeframe. The SVF would also publish each activity on its Facebook, web, Twitter and LinkedIn pages and conduct a weekly live radio

Exploring new concepts and practices   13

programme, acknowledging the Canadian embassy. It also included publishing three newsletters with both online and hard copies.

(F. Amer, personal communication, April 20, 2023)

All these activities publicised and branded the CFLI's financial support through social media, visibility materials such as banners and newsletters, local media coverage and radio programmes. These activities targeted 36,000 women, and citizens benefitted from listening to 36 live radio programmes on women's engagement, the impact of violence on women's empowerment, gender and social responsibility, young women's civic engagement and campaigns to stop violence against women and to protect women from violence.

Social media networks enable CSOs to launch public diplomacy campaigns and share their values and activities (Shea & Lee, 2022). Furthermore, social media campaigns assist CSOs in raising ordinary citizens' voices and making recommendations to different actors and policy-makers. For example, CSOs involved in women's empowerment and fighting violence against women have launched public diplomacy campaigns via Twitter and Facebook. Such values and themes of human rights-based activities are core to funders' interests (Holm, 2020a).

Active public diplomacy

CSOs are required to share their activities' and projects' "success stories" in accordance with their agreements with their donors. Accordingly, CSOs and diplomatic missions identify their "common narratives and main targets". However, CSOs are involved with bottom-up public diplomacy via grassroots people, ordinary citizens, community leaders and elites. CSOs' engagement with social media to promote the values of human rights might generate both opportunities and challenges, as Shea and Lee (2022) highlighted regarding public diplomacy via Twitter.

Human rights is a core issue for western diplomatic missions abroad to engage with local CSOs active in the field of human rights at various levels, including reporting political violations committed by local authorities or non-state actors, training civil activists or reforming and modernising processes and legislation. Diplomatic representatives thus also engage with the local community on field trips and share their stories on social media platforms such as Twitter and Facebook to promote the values of freedom of expression and the protection of defenders of human rights. Diplomatic missions also set up short-term processes for human rights projects, such as "small grants schemes" (Holm, 2020a).

Diplomatic missions also engage in long-term processes in cooperation with other donors that share the same values called "donors' consortiums". As Holm (2020a) discusses, small grants are a vital tool for

14 *Ibrahim Natil*

embassy staff to engage directly with grassroots CSOs in public diplomacy activities and create soft power. Their term of engagement ranges from 3 months to 12 months. These small grants focus on community activities, such as awareness, training, media, conferences, workshops, seminars, etc. However, a few missions support and finance short-term training for highly selected human rights activists to attend professional centres abroad to learn from western perspectives and culturally oriented approaches and values. As Asad Abu Sharkh says, such activities have been seen as "cultural imperialism" by some activists and intellectuals:

> I do think, and rightly so, that the international donations were not given to help Palestinian women be more resilient or steadfast; rather, the true goal was to penetrate Palestinian society. These donations were only given to organise workshops of importance to our society. These donations were of marginal value as they never contributed to building any kind of infrastructure. In addition, these donations tried to distract people's attention from the ominously-agreed goal, i.e., the struggle to end the occupation, because the freedom of Palestinian women can only be achieved through the freedom of Palestine.
> (A. Abu Sharkh, personal communication, September 17, 2020)

Diplomatic missions from Denmark, Sweden, Switzerland and the Netherlands, however, institutionalised and sponsored a long-term joint-donor programme named "The Human Rights and IHR Secretariat" to contribute to the effective realisation of and adherence to human rights and international law. The Secretariat (2013–2017) operated to support human rights and international law NGOs operating in the occupied Palestinian territories. The diplomatic missions of these countries did not engage directly with the CSOs but delegated third parties, such as Birzeit University and Niras Natura, to manage the Secretariat. The Secretariat succeeded in funding a local project (\$ 94,325.00) from December 2015 to November 2016, implemented by the SVF. The project advocated the rights of displaced families who lost their homes in the Israeli bombardments during the summer of 2014, raising the voices and demands of these people to rebuild and return them to their homes. Its activities also engaged the national and international media to raise the concerns of displaced people with various decision-makers and relevant organisations by conducting public debate activities, including hall town meetings, focus groups, local and regional conferences and high-level meetings (F. Amer, Personal Communications, April 20, 2023).

Public diplomacy tools were employed to raise the concerns and demands of these families who lost their houses at the national and international levels. The Human Rights and IHR Secretariat's report (grant agreement number 12/2015-03-PF-37, implemented by the SVF)

Exploring new concepts and practices 15

indicated that a local network of at least 50 CSOs campaigned to influence decision-makers from the public and international and local organisations to fulfil the demands of vulnerable families, children, women and the elderly. This project involved international advocacy activities, national network meetings, field research, town hall meetings, radio productions and broadcasts and conferences, and it featured in the international media. The project conducted five public meetings in Europe to raise the voices of displaced communities after they had lost faith in the international community to assist in rebuilding their houses. The project was subsequently highlighted in the international media to reach the global public, including parliamentarians, politicians, academics, journalists, international CSOs and solidarity groups with the Palestinian people.

The soft power of public diplomacy and the influence of the Human Rights and IHR Secretariat came under attack and it was monitored by opposition groups, just as Israel monitors other NGOs. The Human Rights and IHR Secretariat closed in 2017; however, diplomatic missions have continued to support and engage with well-established civil society groups. These groups have contributed to international debates and activism, including exposing the violations of military occupation that resulted in six Palestinian human rights groups' offices being closed, equipment being confiscated and being labelled as "terrorist entities", as Natil discusses in Chapter 8. Such actions have imposed significant challenges and barriers to CSOs' global engagement and public diplomacy.

Barriers to CSOs' public diplomacy

CSOs' level of public diplomacy engagement is continually challenged by various social, political, health and financial barriers owing to local restrictions and global crises. CSOs are controlled by internal and external circumstances as they are part of the society they operate in and are affected by its dynamics and structures (Natil et al., 2020). CSOs are independent organisations in terms of their management, operations and deliveries; however, they do not have the capacity to influence crises, owing to the nature of society and its societal, political and economic systems. Ahmed El Assal and Amr Marzouk discuss youth participation and barriers to public diplomacy further in Chapter 6.

CSOs also attempt to advocate and influence certain issues and events; however, they have very limited power to make drastic changes (Natil et al., 2020). For example, CSOs attempt to accommodate their engagement with respect to conflicts, wars and political turmoil, such as in Lebanon, Libya, Yemen and Palestine. These conflicts and changes always cause a lot of social reactions, including citizen displacements, house destruction and relocations of local CSO staff.

16 *Ibrahim Natil*

Global or national health crises, barriers and challenges have also influenced CSOs' operations and engagement within the scope of public diplomacy (Natil & Pulla, 2022). The rate of gender-based violence was high in Palestine even before COVID-19, but it has increased since the onset of the COVID-19 crisis and limitations on movement. Many CSOs developed mechanism to support victimised vulnerable people such as women by setting up hotlines to provide counselling following abuse and domestic violence, which increased during the pandemic. The impact is exacerbated in contexts of fragility, conflict, refuge, displacement and emergencies where social cohesion is already undermined and institutional capacity and services are limited. Furthermore, CSOs had to consider solid risk mitigation strategies for the safe and effective delivery of programmes in the context of the COVID-19 pandemic in accordance with WHO guidelines and instructions. As Natil previously discussed (Natil, 2021; Natil & Pulla, 2022), the pandemic posed serious problems and barriers to CSOs' public engagement.

COVID-19 risks created and exacerbated vulnerabilities and inequalities and evidenced the need for expanded and responsive humanitarian support, domestic violence support and mental health services from CSOs. Donors also had to reduce their physical engagement with the public and CSOs. However, they continued their cooperation via digital technology and social media platforms to avoid health risks by maintaining social distance and adhering to health regulations imposed around the globe. Natarajan (2014), however, has argued that digital (public) diplomacy should be an integral part of the practice of diplomacy and connect with foreign publics and influence global opinion. Additionally, the COVID-19 pandemic forced governments and their diplomats in the field who used to engage and work with CSOs to rely mainly on social media platforms such as Twitter to communicate foreign policy goals and attempt to construct a strategic narrative (Wang & Xu, 2022).

CSOs responded to the COVID-19 crisis by taking urgent and well-designed actions to continue delivering services to their communities, such as defending women's social and legal rights to reduce the culture of violence by empowering women's engagement in community-based actions. Local Palestinian CSOs, for example, obtained funding from the Canada Feminist Fund (CFF) for 2021–2022, coordinating with Canada's foreign policy values. Local CSOs' engagement was part of a mechanism established through Canada's West Bank & Gaza Field Support Services Project for Palestinians. CSOs' engagement with Canada's values formed part of their efforts to empower women's rights defenders and community grassroots initiatives, such as those the SVF has delivered in Palestine (F. Amer, Personal Communications, April 20, 2023).

CSOs' responses to social, political and health shifts impose massive financial challenges on their operations, including public engagement

Exploring new concepts and practices 17

and diplomacy with all actors. It is not easy to accommodate such surprising changes. Donors' priorities changing or shifting is considered one of the main challenges to CSOs' engagement at the national and international levels. Donors change their priorities, interests and/or intervention policies due to global or regional crises, such as in Ukraine, Syria, Sudan, Libya, Yemen, Palestine and Iraq. CSOs' responses and reactions to calls for proposals, however, are always controlled by the donors' priorities, agenda, requirements and conditions that affect their level of public diplomacy.

References

Alexander, C. (2018). The soft power of development: aid and assistance as public diplomacy activities. In J. Servaes (Ed.), *Handbook of communication for development and social change* (pp. 407–420). Springer.

Al-Tamimi, N., Amin, A., & Zarrinabadi, N. (2023). *Qatar's nation branding and soft power: exploring the effects on national identity and international stance*. Springer.

Asdourian, B. (2022). Civil society diplomacy: characterizing collective and connective actions for a shared cause. *Journal of Communication Management*. 10.1108/JCOM-04-2022-0041

Bherer, L., Dufour, P., & Montambeault, F. (2016). The participatory democracy turn: an introduction. *Journal of Civil Society*, *12*(3), 225–230. 10.1080/1744 8689.2016.1216383

Broś, N. (2017). Public diplomacy and cooperation with non-governmental organizations in the liberal perspective of international relations. *Journal of Education Culture and Society*, *8*(1), 11–22. 10.15503/jecs20171.11.22

Cull, N. (2008). Public diplomacy: taxonomies and histories. *The Annals of the American Academy of Political and Social Science*, *616*(1), 31–54. 10.1177/0002 716207311952

European Commission. (2007). *A glance at EU public diplomacy at work*. Office for Official Publications of the European Communities.

Fanoulis, E., & Revelas, K. (2023). The conceptual dimensions of EU public diplomacy. *Journal of Contemporary European Studies*, *31*(1), 50–62. 10.1 080/14782804.2022.2043836

Garamvölgyi, B., Bardocz-Bencsik, M., & Dóczi, T. (2022). Mapping the role of grassroots sport in public diplomacy. *Sport in Society*, *25*(5), 889–907. 10.1 080/17430437.2020.1807955

Helmers, H. (2016). Public diplomacy in early modern Europe. *Media History*, *22*(3–4), 401–420. 10.1080/13688804.2016.1174570

Holm, N. (2020a). Making the cut: exploring application evaluation and programme accessibility in embassy-based small grant schemes. *Forum for Development Studies*, *47*(2), 327–350. 10.1080/08039410.2020.1739123

Holm, N. (2020b). Street-level diplomacy? Administrator reflections on small grant schemes as a public diplomacy tool. *Diplomacy & Statecraft*, *31*(3), 557–578. 10.1080/09592296.2020.1782678

18 Ibrahim Natil

Lamal, N., & Gelder, K. (2021). Addressing audiences abroad: cultural and public diplomacy in seventeenth-century Europe. *The Seventeenth Century, 36*(3), 367–387. 10.1080/0268117X.2021.1926651

Natarajan, K. (2014). Digital public diplomacy and a strategic narrative for India. *Strategic Analysis, 38*(1), 91–106. 10.1080/09700161.2014.863478

Natil, I. (2021). Introducing challenges to youth civic engagement and local peacebuilding. In I. Natil (Ed.), *Youth civic engagement and local peacebuilding in the Middle East and North Africa: prospects and challenges for community development* (pp. 1–12). Routledge.

Natil, I. (2022). *New leadership of civil society organisations: community development and engagement.* Routledge.

Natil, I., Malila, V., & Sai, Y. (Eds.). (2020). *Barriers to effective civil society organisations: political, social and financial shifts.* Routledge.

Natil, I., & Pulla. V. (2022). Civil society shifts, challenges and responses to COVID-19: Ireland, Scotland and Wales. *Space and Culture, India, 10*(3), 47–56. 10.20896/saci.v10i3.1245

Pamment, J. (2014). Strategic narratives in US public diplomacy: a critical geopolitics. *Popular Communication, 12*(1), 48–64. 10.1080/15405702.2013.868899

Proedrou, F., & Frangonikolopoulos, C. (2012). Refocusing public diplomacy: the need for strategic discursive public diplomacy. *Diplomacy & Statecraft, 23*(4), 728–745. 10.1080/09592296.2012.736339

Shea, C., & Lee, F. (2022). Public diplomacy via Twitter: opportunities and tensions. *Chinese Journal of Communication, 15*(3), 449–462. 10.1080/1754475 0.2022.2081988

Snow, N. (2008). Rethinking public diplomacy. In N. Snow & P.M. Taylor (Eds.), *Routledge handbook of public diplomacy* (pp. 3–11). Routledge.

Song, W., & Fanoulis, E. (2023). Global perspectives on European Union public diplomacy: an introduction. *Journal of Contemporary European Studies, 31*(1), 1–7. 10.1080/14782804.2022.2156486

Wallström, M. (2008, October 6). *Public diplomacy and its role in the EU's external relations.* https://ec.europa.eu/commission/presscorner/detail/en/SPEECH_08_494

Wang, R., & Xu, W. (2022). Hashtag framing and stakeholder targeting: an affordance perspective on China's digital public diplomacy campaign during COVID-19. *Journal of Information Technology & Politics.* 10.1080/19331681. 2022.2096742

Zielińska, K. (2016). Development diplomacy. Development aid as a part of public diplomacy in the pursuit of foreign policy aims: theoretical and practical considerations. *Historia i Polityka, 16*(23), 9–26. 10.12775/HiP.2016.009

3 Historical review of public diplomacy

Milestones for civic engagement and business

Mohammad Al-Mazawdah

Introduction

Diplomatic history is concerned with official peaceful contacts between countries and the factors that drive each of them to establish such contacts. Diplomatic history deals with various nations managing international affairs through diplomatic correspondence, negotiations carried out by ambassadors, preparation for concluding agreements and treaties and solving outstanding problems. Likewise, diplomacy must consider each country's system, rules, provisions and laws.

Diplomatic relations between the Kingdom of Aragon, the Kingdom of Granada and the Hafsid state were established because of their proximity, their mutual interests and the attempt of each kingdom to preserve and expand its lands. The nature of their relations prompted conflicts and wars on the one hand and treaties and peace on the other. The interest of the kings of Aragon in foreign trade translated into an interest in the Kingdom of Granada and North Africa. They considered this region of political, economic and strategic importance to their political and economic kingdom, and the merchants of the maritime states were affiliated with the crown. Additionally, the Kingdom of Aragon had good relations with Tunisia, Bejaia, Tlemcen and Morocco.

This study deals with the historical development of public diplomacy between the Kingdom of Aragon, the Kingdom of Granada and the Hafsid state to shed light on the history of their diplomatic relations and study the role of ambassadors and consuls in diplomatic relations. It relies on documentary sources from the archives of the Kingdom of Aragon contained in the volume *Los documentos árabes diplomáticos del archivo de la corona de Aragón*. The volume includes correspondence and treaties between the kings of Aragon and the kings of states from the Islamic world, such as Egypt, Tlemcen, Fez, Morocco, Tunisia and Granada.

DOI: 10.4324/9781003441465-3

20 *Mohammad Al-Mazawdah*

The development of diplomacy between Granada and Aragon

A treaty was concluded between the kingdoms of Aragon and Granada in May 1295, between the Sultan of Granada Muhammad ibn Yusuf al-Shahr al-Faqih (1272–1302) and King of Aragon Jaime II. The diplomatic relations between Granada and Aragon in the eighth century AH—the fourteenth century AD were characterised by the conclusion of peace treaties, the renewal of treaties, the exchange of ambassadors and messages to confirm the friendship between the two kingdoms. Many peace treaties were signed between the kingdoms of Granada and Aragon. The diplomatic representation between the two parties was in the exchange of ambassadors and the appointment of consuls. As for the exchange of ambassadors, this was done through diplomatic messages carried by the ambassadors to solve some issues and problems between the two kingdoms or to conclude treaties.

Among these issues, for example, piracy of all kinds, including the letter on March 24, 1315 AD, carried by the ambassador of King Jaime II (1291–1327 AD), Suleiman the Israeli, about controlling several livestock in the Al-Bireh region. The letter also included Muharram 3, 723 AH/January 12, 1323, a complaint from Sultan Ismail I (1314–1325 AD) to King Jaime II about piracy against the eyelids of the Kingdom of Granada. One of the ships was intercepted (Masiá de Ros, 1951, doc. 5, pp. 11–12).

As well as from other issues of prisoners, including the letter in Jumada al-Thani May 1324 AD that was carried by the ambassador of King Jaime II, Guillem de Saynuwiya, in which he carried a letter to Sultan Ismail I, it includes several complaints about some prisoners in the city of Balsh (Masiá de Ros, 1951, doc. 7, pp. 16–17). Sometimes, the ambassadors were merchants, such as the letter on August 31, 1336 AD, which was carried by the merchant Luquin Pascalin, which is a message of friendship and confirmation of the friendly relations between the two kingdoms (Masiá de Ros, 1951, doc. 48, pp. 96–97).

Also, many messages were exchanged between the two kingdoms, carried by ambassadors to conclude peace treaties between the two parties. The ambassadors carried gifts, which confirmed the relations of affection and friendship (Masiá de Ros, 1951, doc. 48, pp. 96–97).

The first diplomatic representation at the level of the consul between the kingdoms of Aragon and Granada appeared in a treaty in 1295 AD. Article 8 of the treaty stated, "And that they present a consul in every place of the court and work for them all their revenues" (Masiá de Ros, 1951, doc. 1, pp. 1–2). We notice in this article the use of the word consul, and it seems that it was used at that time, and it was not new, and it has a presence among trade terms, whether Islamic or Christian, and the consul did not have an official capacity. The inclusion of the term in

Historical review of public diplomacy 21

the treaty indicates that it was given an official status. However, Sultan Muhammad bin Yusuf, the famous jurist (1272–1302 AD), specified the duties of this consul. It is only related to commercial transactions. It did not exceed anything else, and this item gave the Christian merchants the right to have the consul decide their commercial problems. This gave them a sense of safety within the kingdom and encouraged them to practice trade within its lands. The consul must proceed according to what the bureaus in the Kingdom of Granada follow in their commercial transactions (Jabbar, 2019, pp. 114–116).

The residence of the consul is the hotel, and this is considered a development in the meaning of the hotel, and there is a connection between the hotel and the consul, so there is no hotel without the presence of a consul. Because the job of the consul is to organise the affairs of the merchants within it and to solve their problems, the King of Aragon appoints the consul. He may be appointed for a certain period or a lifetime, and he constitutes the mediation between the merchants and their countries. He transmits to his country everything related to their affairs and problems (Al-Nashar, 1997, pp. 242–244; Halalsheh, 2021, p. 39).

The consul took the hotels as an essential source for earning money, as he is the biggest beneficiary of it and collects the income. He appoints the accountants of the hotel, such as the clerk of the Diwan al-Bahr and the disposer of the tavern and liquor, and he also looks into legal cases and takes prescribed sums from them (Beazik, 1998, p. 255; Halalsheh, 2021, p. 40). Because he works to complete the signing of the necessary commercial contracts, rents shops, receives their money and monopolises the sale of alcohol to Christian communities, he is also responsible for the bakery's money and takes money from the merchants for storing their goods.

Moreover, Aragon paid attention to its commercial institutions, especially its consuls and subjects in other countries. Hence, the appointment of the consul was sometimes not by the king of Aragon, but rather the matter of his appointment was left to the merchants, and he would be one of their seniors. As for the consuls abroad, their appointment belonged to the king, and in addition to supervising all the affairs of the merchants, they played the court's role in resolving the dispute between the merchants and the captains of the ships (Al-Nashar, 1997, p. 193; Halalsheh, 2021, p. 39).

A hotel is a two- or three-story building, surrounded by a spacious courtyard, used for unloading and loading goods so that the tax and excise official can monitor it (Villani, 2002, p. 137); the ground floor contains the bakery warehouses and stores for the sale of goods and the offices of the consulate (Bernishvik, 1988, p. 664; Beazik, 1998, p. 315); a translator is available for a fee (Villani, 2002, p. 137); a church, private shops, bathrooms and private cafes for the community (Bo Omran,

22 Mohammad Al-Mazawdah

2007, p. 315); the second and third floors were allocated to merchants for rest and overnight stay, and it is surrounded by a high wall (Villani, 2002, p. 137).

Consular diplomacy and subjects in the Hafsid state

The Hafsid Sultans followed a flexible policy based on appeasement and safety. The features of this policy appeared in many diplomatic documents, especially in the correspondence exchanged with Aragon, which confirms the interest of the Hafsids to follow the policy of truce with the forces in the Mediterranean. Despite the irregularities and breaches that occurred in the treaties between the two parties, the Hafsid state attempted to secure its economic interests in the face of the increasing security threats in the Mediterranean (Smairi, 2020, p. 139; Al-Kharabsheh, 2021, pp. 29–30).

Diplomatic representation between Aragon and the Hafsid state at the level of ambassadors was similar to the relations between Aragon and Granada, where the two countries exchanged diplomatic messages that the ambassadors carried to solve many issues, including piracy, captives, taxes, adherence to treaties, requesting compensation for pirated ships and requesting financial assistance from the Hafsid state (Alarcón Santón et al., 1940, doc. 116, p. 249).

It was difficult to determine the period in which consulates began to practice their work in the main ports in Morocco and to represent their country officially (Bourmala, 2017, p. 260). The first appearance of the word consul in Islamic countries on the representative of the Aragonese merchants, as we mentioned earlier, dates back to the end of the thirteenth century in the treaty of May 15, 1296 AD, between the Kingdom of Granada and the Kingdom of Aragon (Jabbar, 2019, p. 113; Al-Kharabsheh, 2021, pp. 35–36). In Aragon, the king appointed the consul by royal decree, either for a limited time or a lifetime (Beazik, 1998, p. 244).

The word consul was mentioned in the relations between Aragon and the Hafsid state in the 1301 AD treaty between the two parties, where Article 26 stipulated that "they shall have a consul or two consuls to preserve their rights and claim them in the court, and to judge between the Christians, the Catalans, and the Aragonese on land and sea" (Alarcón Santón et al., 1940, doc. 116, p. 249).

The treaty gave the King of Aragon the right to appoint a consul for him in Tunisia, and the consul would defend the rights of the Aragonese merchants. The consul could also enter the presence of the King of Tunisia and talk to him about the rights of the Aragonese merchants. The consuls' powers increased with time; after they were initially limited to caring for the interests of merchants and mediating between them and

Historical review of public diplomacy 23

the court (Jabbar, 2019, p. 116), the consul was the mediator between the merchants and their country and between them and the Hafsid authority. He had powers to negotiate with the Hafsid authority and to liberate peaceful commercial treaties and he was entrusted with following up on the financial matters of Tunisia to Aragon and his delegation in the cases of prisoners and their resolution (Beazik, 1998, pp. 246–247; Al-Kharabsheh, 2021, p. 36).

The document indicated in the treaty the demand for the appointment of two consuls and for him to have the right to claim their rights in the diwan and others and to protect and recover commercial interests from the diwan and Muslim merchants and translators. Moreover, this treaty granted the consul the status of the authority of the judge who judges between the Aragonese among themselves and what they had, and his powers included outside the hotel on land and sea (Alarcón Santón et al., 1940, doc. 116, p. 249).

The Islamic Maghreb hotels were the Christians' headquarters and the consuls of each community from Aragon, Genoa and Pisa. They were located in the coastal cities and outside the city, which together form a complex resembling a small city at a distance of half a mile from the sea sure (Bab Al Bahr) (Al-Wazen, 1983, p. 74; Al-Kharabsheh, 2021, p. 38) and are visited by merchants such as Tunisia, Tripoli, Mahdia, Bejaia and Bouna (Mas-Latrie, 1866, p. 92; Al-Kharabsheh, 2021, p. 38), and sometimes in the inner cities such as Constantine (Al-Wazen, 1983, p. 74).

The hotels had employees at the hotel entrances, chosen from the local population. Their job was to monitor the visitors to the hotel. They had the right to refuse any suspected Christian or Muslim person who was not authorised to enter by the consul unless he was accompanied by one of the translators or customs officials (Mas-Latrie, 1866, p. 39; Al-Kharabsheh, 2021, p. 38); police officers were not allowed to enter the hotel; and if one of the resident merchants commits a violation, they must contact the consul to settle the matter (Villani, 2002, p. 138).

The powers of the consul developed, and the so-called diplomatic immunity of the consuls appeared clearly, as well as the responsibility of the consul for judicial matters, and this was evident in the treaty of 1323 AD, as it included Articles 6, 15, 16, 17 and 19. Article 6 of the treaty clarified the appointment of consuls by the King of Aragon in Tunis and Bejaia, and his privileges remained as they were. If there are privileges for other European countries, such as Genoa, then they had the same, and the consul of Bejaia got 20 pesos per month. The consul of Tunisia got 50 pesos per month, paid to him by customs, and the previous financial obligations were paid to the consul of Tunisia and Bejaia (Capmany y de Montpalau, 1974, pp. 83–84).

As for Article 15, the consuls of the King of Aragon and his aides who resided in the lands of the King of Tunisia and Bejaia would not be

24 *Mohammad Al-Mazawdah*

detained or arrested at customs or in any other place for any reason whatsoever (Capmany y de Montpalau, 1974, p. 88). While Article 16 affirmed that it was not permissible to remove any Christian from the areas of influence of the King of Aragon because of debts or another civil or criminal case, the consul would have kept them according to the law. In the absence of the consul, this was implemented through the customs official as usual (Capmany y de Montpalau, 1974, p. 88).

As for Article 17, in any civil or criminal case that took place between the Christians themselves belonging to the King of Aragon within the lands of Tunisia and Bejaia, the Aragonese consul would prosecute them in condemning or exonerating them on behalf of his king, and the King of Tunisia and the King of Bejaia or his officials should not interfere in that. Likewise, under Article 18, in the event of the conversion of any Aragonese merchant to the King of Aragon because of a civil or criminal case, He would not be subjected to any embarrassment by the officials of the King of Tunisia and the King of Bejaia (Capmany y de Montpalau, 1974, p. 88).

Article 19 states that if any case or any crime occurred by a Muslim against a Christian, he would complain about this matter to the consul; and if the case is civil, and the consul knew that, he would not be charged by the ministers of the King of Tunisia and Bejaia before the case is determined as usual (Capmany y de Montpalau, 1974, p. 89). It was noted in Article 6 of the treaty that there were many changes in the privileges and powers of the consul, as the amount of money was specified per month for each consul. The Tunisian consul received 50 pesos per month, and the consul of Bejaia got 20 pesos per month and got the same previous privileges. The consuls of the European cities, especially the Italian ones, were given new privileges. In that case, the consuls of Aragon would have the same privileges, whereas each community had different privileges than the one before it.

In Article 15, the so-called diplomatic immunity appeared, which did not appear previously, as the consuls were given diplomatic immunity to prevent the Hafsid state from imprisoning the consuls or keeping them in custody, even if they committed violations. They had freedom of movement, entry and departure. In Articles 16, 17, 18 and 19, the powers of the consul in the judiciary were expanded, as he was able to consider his Aragonese subjects in civil and criminal cases by trying the Christians among themselves without the intervention of the King of Bejaia and Tunisia, and in the lands of the Hafsid state, as well, as it allowed the consul to monitor cases that a Muslim commits against a Christian until the final decision was issued against him by his officials.

The consul used to take care of the estate of merchants who passed away. He was the one who inspected and collected all the belongings left by the deceased, whether his items or his trade, and kept them in a place

Historical review of public diplomacy 25

under his direct supervision until his family came to collect them. Likewise, when merchants lose their goods at sea due to weather fluctuations or damage to their boats, and if all or some of them sink into the sea, he was the one who received them until the owners came to retrieve them (Jabbar, 2019, p. 117).

Because of all these tasks they undertook and the heavy responsibilities they burdened, the consuls ought to be treated with much respect and esteem. Indeed, they were fortunate in this, as they were granted the right to visit the Sultan once a month, and then it became twice a month (Jabbar, 2019, p. 117). Several servants and employees assisted the consul in performing their duties, including one who was required to be fluent in reading and writing and preferably know more than one language. Likewise, a clergyman carried out church affairs, conducts prayers and other matters that had fallen within the rituals of worship, such as holidays, religious occasions and ceremonies for the burial of the dead (Jabbar, 2019, p. 117).

Since the life of states requires permanent communication with each other, one of the essential tools of communication between states is external representation, and since diplomatic missions are the organs that organise and manage relations between countries, therefore, in the current era, it is not possible to imagine any sovereign country that does not have diplomatic missions or that does not send diplomats to other countries, as that has become the basis of international relations (Muhammad, 2021, p. 271).

At the beginning of the fifteenth century, some changes began to affect diplomacy, especially the consul. The consul became closer to the employee in the state than to the merchant, where he is appointed for a specific period that differs from one country to another. For some it was one year and others are two years, as it became one of the tasks and powers of the consul with time to expand and gain importance in international relations (Jabbar, 2019, p. 116).

At the beginning of the modern era and the collapse of the feudal system based on force and tyranny, and the emergence of the modern nation-state, reference can be made here to the Treaty of Westphalia in 1648, which is considered a new beginning in international relations, because it came with new principles and ideas, including consolidating and confirming permanent diplomatic representation, since the diplomat's mission has become complex, so his role is no longer limited to representing his country and negotiating matters of concern to his country. Instead, he has to follow up and monitor the course of various matters in the country to which he is delegated and to provide his country with everything that he deems to be of particular importance. Likewise, economic developments in Europe ended all isolation of states, and diplomatic relations thus entered into a new development that

26 Mohammad Al-Mazawdah

necessitated the need for a general international organisation of diplomatic relations (Muhammad, 2021, p. 276).

As for financial matters, the diplomatic missions, especially the consul, depend on the financial resources from the trade or the rulers of the country where he resides. It developed as rulers who sent diplomatic missions became paid for their expenses rather than by the countries receiving them. Few diplomats were interested in achieving commercial goals. The consul was responsible for preserving commercial rights and privileges, and the diplomatic envoys who had previously worked as consuls were interested in the commercial situation (Black, 2013, p. 187).

Since the late eighteenth century, diplomacy has come to be understood in Europe in its modern sense, which is the management of relations between states and not concerning the study of diplomatic documents. It has come to require the interests of other powers and an attempt to settle differences. The conference in Vienna in 1815 AD has come to be seen as a first-rate example of realpolitik that distinguished the resumption of diplomacy of the old regime in the nineteenth-century regime. Accordingly, the fact that European countries have become driven mainly by concern for their national security has increased the value of diplomatic skills in understanding security goals and reconciling them in an international system (Black, 2013, pp. 246–248). Moreover, after bilateral diplomatic relations were widespread in the past, they developed in the modern era when collective diplomacy emerged, that is, diplomacy between countries through conferences or international organisations. This type has been known since the founding of the League of Nations until today (Muhammad, 2021, p. 273).

Accordingly, diplomacy in the Middle Ages and modern times focused on war, peace, trade and trade routes. However, in the modern era, the interest in diplomacy has shifted in addition to the emergence of new issues such as food, energy, water, environment, migration and refugees. The means of communication have also evolved from what it was in the past, as it is now easy to hold conversations or correspondence with modern means of communication, such as the Internet, and to hold conferences through these means of communication remotely. In addition, the areas of countries have shrunk after they were prominent in the past. However, after the emergence of independence and secession movements that appeared in the world, the areas of countries became smaller than they were in the past.

Conclusion

This chapter summarises the historical developments of diplomatic work, its importance in the development of business and the relationship of the diplomatic employee from consuls with civil society from merchants and

Historical review of public diplomacy 27

succession. This chapter concludes several results, the most important of which are as follows:

1 The exchange of embassies expanded between the Kingdom of Aragon, Granada and the Hafsid state. This is to resolve some of the thorny issues between the two parties, such as prisoners of war, piracy and the conclusion of treaties. Several messages were received about the prisoners, the request for their release and the prevention of piracy.

2 The consular representation of the Kingdom of Aragon was in Granada and the Hafsid state, with its ports and markets, where he resides in the hotel. The consul had powers, including taking care of the interests of the merchants and acting as a mediator between them and the court and between the merchants themselves in the hotel, as he was responsible for defending their rights at the court and organising their relationship with Muslim merchants, translators and everyone who dealt with Aragonese merchants.

3 The consuls' powers expanded with time, so he was given the status and authority of a judge to adjudicate in cases involving Aragonese subjects.

4 The emergence of the so-called diplomatic immunity did not appear previously, as the consuls were given diplomatic immunity to prevent the Hafsid state from imprisoning the consuls or keeping them in custody.

References

Al-Kharabsheh, S. (2021). *Treaties between the Kingdom of Aragon and the Hafsid State (700–762 AH/1301–1360 AD): a documentary study in the Aragonese archive.* [Unpublished Master's thesis, Yarmouk University, Jordan].

Al-Nashar, M. (1997). The relationship of the Kingdoms of Castile and Aragon with the Mamluk Sultanate (658–741 AH/1260–1341 AD). *Aien for research, humanitarian studies and social studies*, 193–194.

Al-Wazen, A. (1983). *Description of Africa, investigation: Muhammad Hajji and Muhammad Al-Akhdar.* 2nd ed. Dar Al-Gharb Al-Islami.

Alarcón Santón, M.A., García de Linares, R., & González Palencia, A. (Eds.) (1940). *Los documentos árabes diplomáticos del archivo de la corona de Aragón.* Maestre.

Beazik, S. (1995). *Bejaia during the Hafsid era: an economic and social study.* Tunis First University.

Beazik, S. (1998). *Bejaia during the Hafsid era: an economic and social study.* [Unpublished doctoral dissertation, University of Tunis, Tunisia].

Bernishvik, R. (1988). *A history of Ifriqiya in the Hafsid era from the 13th century to the end of the 15th century AD.* Dar Al-Gharb Al-Islami.

Black, J. (2013). *A history of diplomacy.* Reaktion Books.

28   Mohammad Al-Mazawdah

Bo Omran, S. (2007). *History of Algeria in the Middle Ages through sources*. National Center for Studies and Research on the National Movement and the Revolution of November 1, 1954.

Bourmala, K. (2017). *The foreign trade of the central Maghreb in the Mediterranean Basin from the sixth to the ninth century AH*. [Unpublished Master's thesis, University of Oran, Algeria].

Capmany y de Montpalau, A. (1974). *Antiguos tratados de paces y alianzas entre algunos reyes de Aragon y diferentes principes infieles de Asia y Africa, desde el siglo XIII hasta el XV*. Madrid.

Halalsheh, A. (n.d.). *Treaties between the Kingdoms of Aragon and Granada (The Aragonese Archives)*. [Unpublished Master's thesis, Yarmouk University, Jordan].

Jabbar, A. (2019). The consul and consular representation between the Hafsid State and the Christian powers in Western Europe between the fourteenth and sixteenth centuries AD (eighth and tenth Hijri) through Florentine and Aragonese documents. *Université Abdelhamid Mehri Constantine 2 Journal of Arts and Social Sciences, 16*(2), 110–122.

Mas-Latrie, L. de. (1866). *Traités de paix et de commerce et documents divers concernant les relations des chrétiens avec les Arabes de l'Afrique septentrionale au moyen âge*. Plon.

Masiá de Ros, Á. (1951). *La corona de Aragón y los estados del norte de África*. Instituto Español de Estudios Mediterráneos.

Qasimah, M. (2021). Circumstances of the development of diplomacy and the rules regulating it. *Journal of Legal Studies and Research, 6*(2).

Smairi, H. (2020, May). *Hacking from the perspective of the jurists of the Hafsi era between the legitimacy of jihad and the supremacy of interests*. Faculty of Humanities and Social Sciences, Tunis.

Villani, A. (2002). *Tlemcen in the Zayani Era*. Moufm for Publication and Distribution.

4 Public diplomacy and civil society penetration

The new 'scramble for Africa'

Nguh Nwei Asanga Fon

Introduction

The contemporary era has been marked by two significant developments that is reshaping public diplomacy on the African continent: the first is the emergence of global competitors notably China and Russia who are challenging the US-led Liberal World Order (Fidler & Gordon, 2023) and pushing for a multipolar world (Gang, 2023). The second is the growing influence of civil society organisations (CSOs) in Africa (Essoungou, 2013). Public diplomacy has become one of the major mechanisms through which the aforementioned competition is being engaged in Africa, and CSOs constitute vital asset both sides are vigorously trying to court. This chapter looks at the 'New Scramble for Africa', which is a concept used to demonstrate efforts from the custodians of the Liberal World Order (the US, the UK, and the EU) on the one hand, and emerging global powers (China and Russia) on the other, to penetrate and gain influence and support from Africa through public diplomacy.

The New Scramble for Africa

There is a consensus amongst scholars and experts that Africa is currently undergoing what can be termed as a new scramble with both established global powers and emerging powers engaged in a frantic effort to outsmart each other's influence on the continent (Adam, 2018; Ewalefoh, 2022; Poplak, 2016; The Economists, 2019). Alluding to this development, former US National Security Adviser John Bolton once underscored that Africa is becoming a new theatre of 'great power competition' (The Economist, 2019b). In contrast to the 19th Century scramble marked by hard power (coercion), the new scramble is pursued through what Nye (2008: p.95) describes as 'soft power'—'the ability to shape the preferences of others.' Russia's war in Ukraine and the growing tension between China and Taiwan in the Taiwan Strait seem to be morphing into a new 'Cold War' between these two (Russia and China) and the West. These tensions have pushed both sides to seek allies in Africa.

DOI: 10.4324/9781003441465-4

30 Nguh Nwei Asanga Fon

The most prominent tool through which soft power is being pursued in Africa is diplomacy. Statistics from the 'Diplometrics Program' of the University of Denver's Pardee Center for International Futures reveals that over 320 new embassies or consulates were opened in Africa from 2010–2016 (The Economist, 2019b). These diplomatic and consular outposts and the foreign ministries they belong to, are not just engaged in the traditional form of diplomacy (government-to-government) but are increasing involved in public diplomacy (government-to-people). The proliferation and increasing influence of CSOs in Africa has provided a fertile ground for global powers to cultivate public diplomacy on the continent. The approach of liberal democracies and emerging states towards public diplomacy with African CSOs is examined below by comparing the US, UK, and EU, on the one hand, and China and Russia on the other.

United States and public diplomacy with African CSOs

Though the antecedents of US public diplomacy in Africa can be traced back to the Kennedy Administration with the introduction of the Peace Corps programme in 1961, its formal adoption as a key component of US foreign policy and an instrument of its soft power came up in the post-9/11 era when the US sought to boost its global image that had been severely tarnished by the Second Gulf War (2003) and the Global War on Terrorism that ensued. Broś (2017) underscores that public diplomacy became a key tool employed by the State Department to redeem America's image after its post-9/11 military interventions. The State Department recognised the strategic role civil society especially non-governmental organisations (NGOs) could play in this new diplomatic agenda (Ibid.) and sought to involve them in various programmes and initiatives it undertook to promote public diplomacy across the globe. In Africa, the US is actively involved in working with CSOs in its people-to-people diplomatic efforts. The US engagement with African CSOs can be seen in five key areas: funding, capacity-building, partnerships, networking, and advocacy.

Funding is the most prominent domain of public diplomacy engagement between the US and African CSOs given the crucial role it plays in sustaining the activities of the latter. Through its various diplomatic missions on the continent (embassies and consulates), and the United States Agency for International Development (USAID), the United States African Development Foundation (USADF), the US has and continues to provide grants and funding to African CSOs for projects, programmes and capacity-building. Examples abound across the continent. The US Department of State makes available several grants to African CSOs through its various diplomatic missions in Africa. Examples include: the

Africa Regional Democracy Fund (ARDF) grants, the Ambassador's Special Self-Help Fund (SSH), the Public Diplomacy Small Grants Program, and the Julia Taft Refugee Fund.

One of the agencies leading the charge when it comes to US funding to CSOs in Africa is the USAID. In 2021, the USAID alongside the US Department of State provided funding assistance to the tune of \$8.5 billion to a total of 47 states in Sub-Saharan Africa (SSA), and eight regional programmes (USAID, 2023). In Namibia, USAID partnered with faith-based organisations (FBOs), and the Ministry of Women Affairs and Child Welfare to reach out to about 75,000 orphans (who lost their parents from HIV/AIDS), vulnerable children (whose parents or caretakers are themselves HIV-positive), and caregivers with economic empowerment initiatives and community care (USAID, 2021). In 2022, USAID partnered with US-based international NGO GiveDirectly by providing \$2 million to assist agricultural cooperatives in Morocco to recover from the food crisis induced by recent economic shocks (North Africa Post, 2022). In March 2023, the USAID Mission in South Sudan launched a \$43.5 million youth empowerment initiative dubbed 'Youth Corps Service Model' to provide training and mentorship to 500 South Sudanese Youth Corp leaders to enable them to mentor their peers on living productive, healthy, and engaged lives (U.S. Embassy Juba, 2023).

Another major US donor to African CSOs is USADF. Since its inception in 1980, USADF has awarded over 3,960 grants worth over \$265 million to 64 African local implementing partner organisations with an estimated number of two million people impacted directly and ten million indirectly by these grants (USADF, 2021). While the above examples depict a positive engagement between the US and African CSOs in terms of funding, critics believe there are some lapses when it comes to this aspect of US public diplomacy. Dizolele et al (2022) argue that though the US stands out at the global leader in foreign assistance donations (with a total portfolio of \$35.5 billion in overseas development assistance in 2020), and a good portion of its funding attributed to SSA (\$8.5 billion to 47 SSA states and eight regional programmes in 2020), little of these funding goes directly to local and national African CSOs. Sandefur (2022) goes further to point out that despite the Biden Administration's USAID Administrator Samantha Power's pledge to provide at least a quarter of USAID funding directly to local partners in the next four years (from 2021), little has changed on the ground. He points out that in spite of the claim by USAID's mega American implementers of attributing more grants to local organisations through sub-awards, official statistics proves the contrary as American priority still maintain the lion share of contract awards.

The US has also been actively involved in capacity-building initiatives geared towards equipping African CSOs with skills and tools to achieve

32 *Nguh Nwei Asanga Fon*

their objectives, and to network and create mutually beneficial partnerships with their US counterparts. In this regard, the US government has supported training and technical assistance programmes for African CSOs and civil society leaders through USAID and other agencies. This includes programmes such as: Civil Society 2.0, USAID Strengthening Civil Society Globally (SCS Global), Africa Regional Democracy Fund (ARDF), African Women's Entrepreneurship Program (AWEP), and the Mandela Washington Fellowship for Young African Leaders. The Civil Society 2.0 programme was launched in Marrakech, Morocco in 2009 by then US Secretary of State Hillary Clinton as an initiative to strengthen the capacity of NGOs on new technologies and to establish 'a long-term, self-sustaining network of technologists, volunteers and civil society advocates dedicated to promoting the work of civil society in the 21st Century' (Clinton as cited in Broś, 2017: p. 19). Through the SCS Global Program, USAID ran a capacity-building program on health reforms dubbed Citizens' Involvement in Health Governance (CIHG) for Guinean CSOs from July 2017–July 2020; the Boresha Habari/Media and Civil Society Strengthening Activity (TMCS) programme with CSOs and media outlets in Tanzania from August 2017–August 2022; and a two-year 'Civil Society Organizations' Strengthening Program' in Djibouti (USAID, 2018).

Launched in 2010, AWEP has provided training for dozens of women entrepreneurs in Africa (34 at its inaugural edition) and empowered them to become 'voices of change' in their home communities (Devex, 2023). Since its inception in 2014, The Mandela Washington Fellowship for Young African Leaders has provided leadership and academic training to more than 5,800 young leaders (usually CSO or community leaders ages from 25–35) from all 49 SSA countries (Mandela Washington Fellowship, 2023). All the aforementioned programmes also provide ideal networking platforms for African CSOs and their leaders to engage in a mutually beneficial exchange with entities with whom they can collaborate and partner with in the future.

The US government has been actively engaged in advocacy towards the protection and promotion of the rights of CSOs in Africa, which has witnessed increasing onslaughts from various state governments. Musila (2019) revealed that between 2004 and 2018, 12 African countries adopted restrictive laws or policies targeting NGOs. In November 2014, USAID co-sponsored an African regional workshop on the protection of civic space in Africa hosted by the University of Pretoria in South Africa. This workshop came on the heels of the US-Africa Leaders' Summit (bringing together 47 African heads of states) hosted by President Barack Obama in August 2014 during which the trend of closure of civic space in Africa was one of the topics addressed (Ibid.).

The United Kingdom and public diplomacy with African CSOs

There has been a significant decline in the UK's influence and interest in Africa in recent years. Since the collapse of Pax Britannica, and the dawn of independence in Africa in the mid-20th Century, Britain's influence and interest in Africa seems to have witnessed a sharp decline. Experts believe the political and economic gap between the UK and Africa has widened in recent years (Pantuliano & Mendez-Parra, 2022). Geopolitically and geostrategically, Britain is not keen to rekindle its hegemonic influence over the region. The UK's bilateral assistance to African countries witnessed a colossal 66% cut in 2021 as London narrowed the scope of its international development engagement and reprioritised its focus from poverty reduction to climate change (Usman & Glennie, 2022).

The aforementioned notwithstanding, London has also been actively engaged in public diplomacy with CSOs in Africa. Though significantly lower in scale than that of the US, the UK has and continues to support African CSOs. This support has been channelled principally through the Department of International Development (DFID) and the Foreign and Commonwealth Office (FCO), which were merged in September 2020 to form the Foreign, Commonwealth and Development Office (FCDO). Britain's public diplomacy engagement with African CSOs can be seen in two principal domains: funding, and capacity-building.

In 2014, the DFID launched UK Aid Direct, a £150 million programme that seeks to provide direct assistance to CSOs in the UK and overseas. So far, UK AID Direct has funded CSO projects in 23 African countries (UK Aid Direct, 2021). From the empowerment and education of young women with 'Hay2Timbuktu' in Timbuktu, Mali; the facilitation of the education of children suffering from cerebral palsy in Ghana; the prevention of identity-based gender violence in the Great Lake regions (Burundi, Central African Republic, Kenya, Uganda, Tanzania, United Republic of, Zambia); the reduction of TB and HIV/TB co-infection related morbidity and mortality in Zimbabwe's Manicaland Province; and the launch of an urban sanitation city data hub in Madagascar's capital Antananarivo (Ibid), UK Aid Direct funded projects have made direct impact on resident communities in Africa. Alas, like the case with USAID funding, a sizeable portion of UK Aid Direct grants are awarded to UK registered charities. 88% (112 out of 127) of all the grants awarded by UK Aid Direct in 23 African Countries from 2014–March 2021 were given to UK registered charities, only 7% (9 out of 127) were awarded to African CSOs.

Another challenge has been the reduction of UK overseas development assistance (ODA) budget from 0.7% to 0.5% of the country's gross national income in 2021. Despite a statement signed by 85 international and local NGOs and supported by the South Sudan NGO Forum

34 *Nguh Nwei Asanga Fon*

(comprising 400 national and 120 international NGOs), calling on the British government to reconsider its international assistance cuts, which is vital to their activities (NRC, 2021), the British government went ahead with a 66% cut in individual aid to African countries (Wintour & McVeigh, 2021).

Another domain where the UK provides assistance to African CSOs is capacity-building. The biggest success story is undoubtedly the Strengthening Transparency, Accountability and Responsiveness in Ghana (STAR-Ghana) five-year programme (October 2015–October 2021) co-funded by the DFID. STAR-Ghana provided technical assistance and built the capacity of Ghanaian CSOs on citizen rights advocacy, monitoring and evaluation. The programme was so successful that it was transformed into a Ghanaian-owned and led entity in 2019 (Social Development Direct, 2020).

The European Union and public diplomacy with African CSOs

The EU's interest in Africa has witnessed a significant increase since the beginning of the new millennium. The Africa-EU partnership formally saw the light of day in 2000 as the offspring of the maiden Africa-EU Summit that was held in Cairo in the same year (African Union, 2023). This partnership ushered an institutional framework for public diplomacy between the EU and Africa with the inclusion of a 'people-centred partnership' between civil society and non-state actors in the Joint Africa-EU Strategy (JAES) adopted at the second Africa-EU Summit in 2007 (European Commission, n.d.). In Article 107 of the JAES document, both parties undertook to 'further promote the development of a vibrant and independent civil society and of a systematic dialogue between it and public authorities at all levels.'

African CSOs constitute an integral part of this new partnership which has witnessed the holding of three joint EU-Africa civil society fora (Lisbon in 2007; Tunis in 2017; and Brussels in 2022) by representatives of African and European CSOs at the margins of the Africa-EU Summits. Generally, there has also been a giant increase in EU funding towards Africa as a part of a strategy to counter China's charm offensive on the continent. In 2022, the EU earmarked the sum of 150 billion euros for its African investments as part of its efforts to provide an alternative to funds from China on the continent (Reuters, 2022). EU public diplomacy engagement with African CSO can be dissected under two key areas: funding, and capacity-building and networking.

The EU funds African CSOs through the following institutional platforms: the European Development Fund (EDF), the European Neighbourhood Instrument (ENI) and the European Instrument for Democracy and Human Rights (EIDHR). Access to EDF funding was

Public diplomacy and civil society penetration 35

opened to CSOs in Africa through the 'Contonou Agreement' between the EU and African, Caribbean and Pacific (ACP) countries, signed in 2000. Under the Cotonou Agreement, African CSOs can have access to up to 15% of the total EDF funds allocated to an ACP member country (Ibid). At a summit on migration in Valletta in November 2015, the EU established the EU Trust Fund (EUTF) for Africa under the EDF to address the root causes of irregular migration from the continent and contribute to a better management of the phenomenon in three sub-regions of the continent—Sahel/Lake Chad; North Africa, and Horn of Africa. The EUTF has a total budget of 5 billion euros out of which 254 projects worth 4.9 million euros, targeting 25 African countries, have already been approved for execution by diverse categories of implementers among which are African CSOs (Ibid).

The ENI has a 'Southern Civil Society Facility' which is specifically in charge of managing funding to CSOs in partner countries of ENI South which include five North African countries—Algeria, Morocco, Tunisia, Libya, and Egypt (European Union, 2023; Concorde Europe, 2020). In 2015, the ENI provided grants to the tune of 3,222,222 euros to CSOs from ENI South countries through the 'Neighbourhood South Civil Society Facility 2015' (European Commission, 2015). The ENI currently funds the 'Safir' project (2020–2024) with a budget of 7,08 million euros which provides support to 21 CSOs in ENI South to enhance their methodologies on advocacy training (European Union, 2023b).

The EIDHR has been a vital mechanism through which the EU has provided assistance to African CSOs. The EIDHR, which ran from 2014–2020, was peculiar at two levels: first, its ability to fund CSO directly without needing an approval from the host government; and second, the fact that it awarded a greater portion of its grants (45%) to local CSOs (Youngs, n.d.). In Nigeria, the EIDHR provided 15 million euros grant to the 'Agents for Citizen-driven Transformation (ACT)' programme which sought to enhance the credibility of Nigerian CSOs and enhance their role as independent development actors and agents of change. After the Arab Spring, the EIDHR provided funding of two million euros and one million euros respectively in 2011, and 2012 to Tunisian CSOs under the EIDHR Country Based Support Scheme (EESC, 2016).

From the above discussion, it is glaring that the EU has made significant contributions in providing financial assistance to African CSOs. However, there has been some criticism about the conditionalities attached to some EU instruments like the EUTF which has recently been oriented more towards security and conflict resolution rather than poverty reduction which is the main concern of most African CSOs. Reacting to the shift of priorities in the EUTF, an international NGO representative working in Burkina Faso underscored:

36 *Nguh Nwei Asanga Fon*

When donors tie development efforts of NGOs to anti-terrorism, security or conflict resolution it directly threatens the humanitarian principle of neutrality to which NGOs abide. The EUTF is a good mechanism, yet it's polluted by politics. We don't want NGOs to be associated with the fight against illegal migration or terrorism.

(Boduel et al, 2019; p. 4)

Another area in which the EU has been active in its public diplomacy towards African CSOs is capacity-building and networking. Many of the projects funded by grants from EU mission in several African countries are geared towards training and capacity-building of local CSOs. Good examples include: four training courses for youth organisations belonging to the Africa-Europe Civil Society Forum (Tarrafal 2002, Coimbra 2005, Almada 2006, and Mollina 2014) organised by the Council of Europe's North-South Centre (Council of Europe, 2023); and the 4.75 million euros ENI 'Thaqafa Daayer Maydoor (All-Around Culture)' capacity-building project that covers CSOs from Egypt, Morocco, Tunisia, Algeria, and Libya among other countries of ENI South (European Union, 2022).

One of the jewels of the EU's public diplomacy engagement with African CSOs is undoubtedly the African-EU Civil Society Forum establish within the framework of the JAES to be a networking forum par excellence that brings together African and European CSOs. The forum is supported by the EU and the African Union (AU) and has held three sessions as mentioned above. On a general note, liberal powers have been more intentional, effective, and efficient in their support to African CSOs. According to Afiniki Mangzha, Executive Director of a Nigerian CSO dubbed Integrated Women and Youth Empowerment Center (IYWEC), the US, UK, and EU, through their diplomatic missions in Nigeria, have provided project funding, and capacity-building programmes to Nigerian CSOs on issues such as: the promotion of human rights and democracy; conflict management; gender equality; education and empowerment (Fon, 2023). Mangzha also believes the engagement of the aforementioned countries with Nigerian CSOs have left a good impression in the minds of the latter about the former (Ibid.).

Emerging/Revisionist powers and civil society engagement in Africa

Russia and China have remained relatively inactive when it comes to public diplomacy engagement with African CSOs. Though they have recently been presenting themselves as counterweights and alternatives to the US-led liberal order, both countries have a more state-centric diplomatic approach towards Africa. Engagement with CSOs goes against the grain of their totalitarian approach to leadership. A thriving

Public diplomacy and civil society penetration 37

civic space is in the DNA of democratic societies but antithetical to regimes that perceive CSOs and the civil society as a whole as a threat to their domestic and foreign policy objectives. Cheeseman (2002) sums it up nicely in the following terms:

> One reason for the comparative lack of Chinese and Russian engagement in funding NGOs to date may be that domestically, Beijing and Moscow tend to see civil society groups as a threat and something to be contained and, hence, to have less established routes of pushing funding to civic organisations.

Russia and China's public diplomacy with African CSOs

So far, Moscow and Beijing have not pursued any formal public diplomacy engagement with African CSOs. Russian public diplomacy engagement with Africa has been concentrated predominantly on educational and cultural exchanges with about 15,000 African students (mostly from Angola, Tunisia, Nigeria, and Morocco) studying in Russian universities as of 2021 (Siegle, 2021). China on its part has focused its efforts mostly on promoting its cultural diplomacy. As of 2021, China had collaborated with African countries to establish a total of 61 Confucius Institutes and 48 Confucius classrooms in the region. It has also assisted 30 African universities to put in place a department of Chinese language or a Chinese language major, and sent out a total of 5,500 Chinese language instructors and volunteers to a total of 48 African states (Ibid.). While providing support to CSOs and naturing civic space in Africa may not tie with their totalitarian DNA, it is possible that Russia and China may become pragmatic in the future and selectively offer support to some African CSOs that are willing to embrace and represent their interest in the continent.

Conclusion

In recent times, Africa has once again become the theatre of a scramble for its control among major global powers; this time not with the coercive arm of colonialism but with the attractive force of public diplomacy. As key actors in the African socio-political landscape, CSOs have attracted the attention and engagement of most of the foreign power seeking to extend their influence on the continent. This chapter probed into the public diplomacy engagement of the various major powers involved in the new scramble for Africa. It contrasted the efforts made by liberal powers (US, UK, and EU) and revisionist powers (China and Russia) to rally African CSOs behind their cause. It was revealed that liberal powers have an overwhelming advantage over their

38 Nguh Nwei Asanga Fon

revisionist counterparts when it comes to engagement with African CSOs given their enduring commitment to the latter in terms of providing funding, capacity-building and networking opportunities, as well as advocacy. Some lapses in the engagement of liberal powers with African CSOs like the lopsided allocation of grants in favour of Western CSOs, and their reprioritisation of grants towards security at the expense of poverty reduction were pointed out. In conclusion, it would be a gross miscalculation for liberal powers to lie on their laurels given the current favourable dynamics in their public diplomacy with African CSOs. Revisionist powers are well able and capable of conceiving and implementing strategies to reverse the tide.

References

Adam, A. (2018). Are we witnessing a 'new scramble for Africa'? Retrieved April 17, 2023, from https://www.aljazeera.com/opinions/2018/3/27/are-we-witnessing-a-new-scramble-for-africa

African Union. (2023). Retrieved from https://au.int/en/partnerships/africa_eu

Boduel, C., Jaymond, M., Rivalan, B., & Voitzwinkler, F. (2019). Retrieved from https://www.ghadvocates.eu/wp-content/uploads/policy_brief_donor_interests_FINAL_web.pdf

Broś, N. (2017). Public diplomacy and cooperation with non-governmental organizations in the liberal perspective of international relations. *The Journal of Education, Culture, and Society, 8*(1), 11–22.

Cheeseman, N. (2002). Retrieved from https://carnegieeurope.eu/2022/11/30/african-civil-society-and-external-influences-that-shape-it-pub-88481

Council of Europe. (2023). Retrieved from https://www.coe.int/en/web/north-south-centre/capacity-building-activities

CONCORD Europe. (2020). Retrieved from https://concordeurope.org/wp-content/uploads/2016/08/guide_to_europeaid_funding_instruments_2014-2020.pdf

Devex. (2023). African Women's Entrepreneurship Program (AWEP) | Devex. Retrieved April 27, 2023, from https://www.devex.com/organizations/african-women-s-entrepreneurship-program-awep-54339

Dizolele, M., Kurtzer, J., & Abdullah, H. (2022). Localizing Humanitarian Action in Africa. Retrieved April 26, 2023, from https://www.csis.org/analysis/localizing-humanitarian-action-africa

EESC. (2016). Retrieved from https://webapi2016.eesc.europa.eu/v1/documents/eesc-2015-00659-00-01-ri-tra-et.docx/content

Essoungou, A.. (n.d.). Retrieved from https://international-partnerships.ec.europa.eu/policies/africa-eu-partnership_en

Essoungou, A. (2013). The rise of civil society groups in Africa | Africa Renewal. Retrieved April 11, 2023, from https://www.un.org/africarenewal/magazine/december-2013/rise-civil-society-groups-africa

European Union. (2023). Retrieved from https://south.euneighbours.eu/project/safir/

Public diplomacy and civil society penetration 39

European Union. (2023b). Retrieved from https://south.euneighbours.eu/the-european-neighbourhood-instrument-eni/

European Union. (2022). Retrieved from https://south.euneighbours.eu/project/thaqafa-daayer-maydoor-all-around-culture/

European Commission. (2015). Retrieved from https://neighbourhood-enlargement.ec.europa.eu/system/files/2017-04/4_c_2015_6146_f1_annex_en_v1_p1_814974.pdf

Ewalefoh, J. (2022). The New Scramble for Africa. *The Palgrave Handbook of Africa and the Changing Global Order*, 309–322.

Fidler, S., & Gordon, M. R. (2023). Russia, China Challenge U.S.-led World Order. Retrieved April 11, 2023, from https://www.wsj.com/articles/russia-china-challenge-u-s-led-world-order-3563f41d

Fon, N. N. A. (2023, April29). Interview With Ms. Afiniki Mangzha Executive Director, Integrated Women and Youth Empowerment Centre (IWAYEC). personal.

Gang, Q. (2023). A Journey of Friendship, Cooperation and Peace that Attracts Worldwide Attention —State Councilor and Foreign Minister Qin Gang on President Xi Jinping's State Visit to Russia. Retrieved April 11, 2023, from https://www.fmprc.gov.cn/mfa_eng/zxxx_662805/202303/t20230324_11048606.html#:~:text=China%20and%20Russia%20are%20committed,a%20shared%20future%20for%20mankind

Mandela Washington Fellowship. (2023). Mandela Washington Fellowship for Young African Leaders. Retrieved April 27, 2023, from https://www.mandelawashingtonfellowship.org/

Musila, G. (2019). The spread of Anti-NGO measures in Africa: Freedoms under threat. Retrieved April 27, 2023, from https://freedomhouse.org/report/special-report/2019/spread-anti-ngo-measures-africa-freedoms-under-threat

North Africa Post. (2022). Morocco: USAID & GiveDirectly NGO support agricultural cooperatives with $4 Mln Funding. Retrieved April 26, 2023, from https://northafricapost.com/61711-morocco-usaid-givedirectly-ngo-support-agricultural-cooperatives-with-4-mln-funding.html

NRC. (2021). NGOs ask the UK government not to cut aid to South Sudan as threat of famine looms. Retrieved April 29, 2023, from https://www.nrc.no/news/2021/march/re-ngos-ask-the-uk-government-not-to-cut-aid-to-south-sudan-as-threat-of-famine-looms/

Nye Jr, J. S. (2008). Public diplomacy and soft power. *The Annals of the American Academy of Political and Social Science*, *616*(1), 94–109.

Pantuliano, S., & Mendez-Parra, M. (2022). UK-Africa Relations: The need for an urgent reset. Retrieved April 29, 2023, from https://www.brookings.edu/blog/africa-in-focus/2022/02/15/uk-africa-relations-the-need-for-an-urgent-reset/

Poplak, R. (2016). The New Scramble for Africa: How China became the partner of choice. Retrieved April 17, 2023, from https://www.theguardian.com/global-development-professionals-network/2016/dec/22/the-new-scramble-for-africa-how-china-became-the-partner-of-choice

Reuters. (2022). Retrieved from https://www.reuters.com/world/africa/eu-earmarks-150-billion-euros-investment-africa-2022-02-10/

Sandefur, J. (2022). USAID localization by the numbers. Retrieved April 26, 2023, from https://www.cgdev.org/blog/usaid-localization-numbers

40 *Nguh Nwei Asanga Fon*

Siegle, J. (2021). Retrieved from https://africacenter.org/experts/joseph-siegle/russia-strategic-goals-africa/

Social Development Direct. (2020). Strengthening transparency accountability and responsiveness phase 2 (Star-Ghana). Retrieved April 29, 2023, from https://www.sddirect.org.uk/project/strengthening-transparency-accountability-and-responsiveness-phase-2-star-ghana

The Economist. (2019). The New Scramble for Africa. Retrieved April 17, 2023, from https://www.economist.com/leaders/2019/03/07/the-new-scramble-for-africa

The Economist. (2019b). Africa is attracting ever more interest from powers elsewhere. Retrieved April 17, 2023, from https://www.economist.com/briefing/2019/03/07/africa-is-attracting-ever-more-interest-from-powers-elsewhere

U.S. Embassy Juba. (2023). U.S. government launches USAID Youth Empowerment Activity in western bahr el ghazal, South Sudan. Retrieved April 26, 2023, from https://ss.usembassy.gov/youth-empowerment-activity-wau-230330/

UK Aid Direct. (2021). About UK Aid Direct /Where we work. Retrieved April 29, 2023, from https://www.ukaiddirect.org/about/where-we-work/

USADF. (2021). Supporting African-led Solutions to Create Pathways to Prosperity. Retrieved April 26, 2023, from https://www.usadf.gov/celebrating-40-years

USAID. (2023). Bureau for Africa: Organization. Retrieved April 26, 2023, from https://www.usaid.gov/about-us/organization/bureau-africa

USAID. (2021). Global health: Namibia. Retrieved April 26, 2023, from https://2017-2020.usaid.gov/namibia/global-health

USAID. (2018). Strengthening Civil Society Globally. Retrieved April 27, 2023, from https://pdf.usaid.gov/pdf_docs/PA00XGK6.pdf

Usman, Z., & Glennie, J. (2022). Sign of the Times: How the United Kingdom's Integrated Review Affects Relations with Africa. Retrieved April 29, 2023, from https://carnegieendowment.org/2022/02/22/sign-of-times-how-united-kingdom-s-integrated-review-affects-relations-with-africa-pub-86484

Wintour, P., & McVeigh, K. (2021). African countries facing 66% cut in UK aid, charities say. Retrieved April 29, 2023, from https://www.theguardian.com/politics/2021/apr/28/african-countries-facing-66-cut-in-uk-aid-charities-say

Youngs, R. (n.d.). Retrieved from https://www.hss.de/download/publications/AA_92_EU-Unterstuetzung_englisch.pdf

5 Being at the forefront

Polish CSOs' contribution to public diplomacy and development cooperation efforts

Galia Chimiak and Katarzyna Zalas-Kamińska

Introduction

This chapter focuses on the challenges and opportunities CSOs have faced while implementing projects in the fields of public policy, development cooperation and democratisation assistance. It also discusses aspects of Polish CSOs' involvement (countries, topics, types of programmes and campaigns) and the dimensions of their activities. By focusing on the distinctive characteristics of Polish CSOs and their cooperation with national and international stakeholders, including their work with Ukrainian partners prior to the ongoing war in Ukraine, the paper will seek to elucidate Polish CSOs' potential to impact political and social life at home as well as abroad, as well the most distinctive issues they face with regard to enhancing their own social power at home and impact on developments abroad. While recognising that, as the government's partners, those CSOs have been realising Polish public diplomacy goals, which are determined by the country's foreign policy priorities, this chapter will present evidence that CSOs' engagement in public policy, development cooperation and democratisation projects has simultaneously been a way of building their own capacity, which has accordingly increased their role in both national and international affairs.

In this chapter, Civil Society Organisations (CSOs) are understood as "self-organised associations that engage in collective action that crosses state boundaries" (Hochstetler, 2015: 177). Also more commonly known as Non-Governmental Organisations, these entities' first legal definition dating back to 1945 explicitly refers to their function in international relations, including their participation in consultation processes with the United Nations (Martens, 2002: 271). CSOs' ever increasing role in international relations envisages a range of fields where they strive to shape global politics and impact societal norms, including research, education, advocacy and lobbying, agenda setting but also to deliver services

DOI: 10.4324/9781003441465-5

42 Galia Chimiak and Katarzyna Zalas-Kamińska

and humanitarian aid, act as watchdogs to help implement international commitments, or engage in direct action (Cooper et al., 2015: 10). In the field of social diplomacy, CSOs are argued to exhibit equal or higher level of capacity, know-how and accountability than the state (Surmacz, 2014: 54). CSOs are furthermore considered to have greater credibility internationally than national governments (Zatepilina-Monacell, 2012). This argument refers to cases where norm-induced change is concerned, i.e. when states are the ones to follow in the steps of CSOs in transforming the international system (Schmitz & Sikkink, 2008: 522).

Theoretical considerations

Even though both public diplomacy and development cooperation efforts keep being coordinated and predominantly funded by governmental stakeholders, CSOs' seminal role not as mere implementers but as "policy entrepreneurs" (Adler, 2008: 104) has been established especially in constructivist thinking. Constructivists highlight the role of norms and ideas in impacting international and domestic policy outcomes alike (Schmitz & Sikkink, 2008: 521) while taking stock of the growing role of non-state actors like CSOs in world affairs.

Certainly, constructivism is not the sole theoretical approach applied to explain the critical role CSOs play internationally. A theoretical lens that highlights the unintended side-effects of CSOs' involvement in cultural diplomacy is Pierre Bourdieu's field theory conceptualised as "an asymmetrically constituted space of power relations, hence of unspoken competition and conflict in a "game" that agents play" with the aim to enhance their economic, social and cultural capital (Isar, 2022: 244). CSOs' function in international cultural diplomacy can therefore be understood as a soft tool that sometimes inadvertently legitimises established power relations, where structural inequalities could lead to paternalistic relations.

These reservations notwithstanding, it is worthwhile to focus on CSOs contribution to public diplomacy and development cooperation alike especially in the case of more recent donors. This choice is not justified solely by the motivation to make up for the existing gap in the literature, but also by the intention to highlight the benefits that post-socialist donors unencumbered by colonial history have brought to the reformulation of norms and practices in the international arena. In view of the ongoing war of the Russian Federation against Ukraine, the recent public recognition that the concerns of Eastern European states like Poland were not sufficiently heeded[1], further corroborates the need to bring to the attention of the academic community the reasoning behind Poland's ongoing support for democratisation to the East and Polish aid's long-term assistance for the civil societies in post-Soviet, non-EU states, especially Belarus and Ukraine (Pisarska, 2008: 7).

Being at the forefront 43

New donors' perspective

Therefore in this chapter, in line with constructivist theorising that attributes the global norm diffusion in the area of human rights to CSOs networks (Schmitz & Sikkink, 2008: 531), we focus on the role of Polish CSOs involved in development cooperation and public diplomacy efforts. The said roles are: project implementation, education, initiation of debates and awareness raising. As hinted above, the choice of Poland as a case study is justified not only in view of the until recently commonly held observation that the focus of aid programs of most European Union (EU) members states that joined since 2004 diverged from the priorities established by the 15 "old" EU MS (Lightfoot, 2010). The Visegrad countries' limited involvement in Africa and their focus on transferring their experience with democratic and economic transitions to neighbouring countries used to be dismissed as their communist legacy and lack of strategic vision in foreign policy (Kopiński, 2012). After the EU enlargement in 2004, an increase of interest in Eastern issues within the EU was observed along with a "mental change in the perception of the Region" by the 15 "old" EU MS (Pisarska, 2008: 6). That Poland has undertaken democracy promotion – in the words of the then minister of foreign affairs Radosław Sikorski as a "Polish priority and a Polish brand"– has been demonstrated in the continuing support of Polish aid and Polish CSOs for Ukrainian partners. With the advantage of hindsight, it can be seen now that the democratisation assistance for post-Soviet states has not been less urgent than the support targeting traditional development partners in the Global South. This chapter will therefore discuss the comparative advantage of CSOs from countries which evolved from beneficiaries of official aid to donors on the example of Poland.

This chapter furthermore brings together two studies of Polish CSOs, i.e. one focusing on CSOs engaged in public diplomacy and the other – on development cooperation, democratisation assistance, humanitarian aid and global education. Even though traditionally those two fields of inquiry have been conducted separately, the benefits coming from their joint study have been highlighted recently (Pamment, 2016). Public diplomacy is thought of being of either informational or relational type, and development aid programs belong to the latter (Zaharna, 2009). In fact, both public diplomacy and development cooperation are examples of *soft power*, defined as "the ability to get what you want through attraction rather than coercion or payments" (Nye, 2004: 5). Among other scholars, James Pamment contended that the growing importance of CSOs has impacted the way of conducting diplomacy (2013: 26-27).

These trends have been recognised in developed countries' foreign policies, for example state-CSOs cooperation in public diplomacy in the

44 Galia Chimiak and Katarzyna Zalas-Kamińska

USA (Broś, 2017). As far as Poland is concerned, even though the first publication concerning the potential of Polish CSOs international activity came out twenty years ago (Czubek, 2002), research on Polish CSOs' contribution to public diplomacy and development cooperation alike has so far seldom been a subject of scholarly attention. There have been studies describing the beginnings of Polish CSOs' involvement abroad (Stanowski, 2002), including their support for countries-recipients of development aid, dealing with democratisation assistance to Eastern European states, regarding the management of foreign aid in Poland (Drążkiewicz, 2020), or analysing Polish CSOs' role in global education (Jasikowska, 2018). This chapter is based on Galia Chimiak's research on Polish developmental CSOs' impact on Polish Aid (Chimiak, 2016) and on Katarzyna Zalas-Kamińska's study of Polish CSOs' role in public diplomacy (Zalas-Kamińska, 2019).

Polish CSOs' role in development cooperation

The role of Eastern European dissidents in the 1980s for the revival of interest in civil society has been well-documented. As far as the internationalisation of Polish civil society goes, it can be traced back to the *Message of the First Congress of NSZZ "Solidarity" Delegates to the Working People in Eastern Europe* adopted at the first Congress of the trade union Solidarity in September 1981. That message underscored the community of experiences of the working people in the then communist countries. Importantly, the document eventually led to the demand for the introduction of martial law in Poland by the then Soviet Communist Party leader Leonid Brezhnev, because it was interpreted as a threat. As an aid professional engaged in a Polish developmental CSO claimed, the "*ideational roots*" of the contemporary international engagement of Polish civil society derive from that message, as post-1989 Polish CSOs' insistence on sharing the "*democratic know-how*" abroad has been a result of the "*messianic conviction that the skills we acquired should be further transferred. This is the mission of Polish civil society, which goes back to the Solidarity ethos*"[2]. Poland started to receive significant US assistance as early as the 1980s, because "the Polish corridor was the West's entry point to the region" (Sussman, 2010: 127).

Naturally, it was after 1989 that Polish CSOs started receiving significant foreign aid from public and private donors alike. Other than the purely financial aspect of this assistance, CSOs in Poland became exposed to new progressive ideas, many of which were novel to Eastern Europe. This cooperation contributed to the internationalisation of Polish CSO activities, too. The examples of the Helsinki Foundation for Human Rights or the then Nobody's Children Foundation, which began

Being at the forefront 45

cooperating with other post-communist countries to share the know-how they gained via their cooperation with Western partners, are cases in point. After the toppling of the previous regime, Janina Ochojska of the Polish Humanitarian Action organised the first convoy of humanitarian aid to war-torn Sarajevo in 1992. The first official Polish aid projects took place in 1998 (Gruca, 2011: 36). Krzysztof Stanowski's account of the history of Polish CSOs engagement abroad merits attention here (Stanowski, 2002). The first of the three stages of this process lasted from 1989 until 1994 and was characterised by Polish CSOs' utilising foreign aid and learning from Western CSOs while establishing their first contacts with neighbouring countries. The second stage took place from 1995 until 1999, and paved the way for the long-term transnational involvement of Polish CSOs. After 1999, the third stage was characterised by a "rapid boom" of transnational CSOs' cooperation, including a growing number of smaller local CSOs which started implementing projects abroad (Ibid.).

Importantly, as a contemporary of the described events recalled, CSOs' culture of cooperation initially diverged from that of the governments, as "*whereas at the onset of the democratic transition, in 1988–89, Poland politically aspired after the West ... we [Polish NGOs] used to cooperate with the Lithuanians, Ukrainians, the Crimean Tatars*". In a way, Polish CSOs – while being recipients of foreign aid themselves – were exposed to two different approaches to democracy assistance. Whereas the United States' policy has been largely political as it focused on supporting citizens' participation in democratic political processes, the European Union prioritised socio-economic development over the support for political openness (Pospieszna, 2014: 33). An interviewed aid professional recalled that when Poland joined the EU said:

"The EU pushed us in the direction of development [cooperation], whereas those of us who have been previously trained by the Americans in the 1980s and the 1990s, didn't have the experience to support development without taking into account [the enhancing of] democratisation and [civic] liberties; we found it natural that there could be no development without democracy... . But the EU back then, due to the attack of the US on Iraq, persisted [in supporting development], and democracy promotion became a pejorative term".

When analysing Poland's multiannual development cooperation programmes, it becomes evident that Polish bilateral aid has placed greater emphasis on political support to partner countries than to classical developmental assistance. Back in 2010, Andrew Curry argued that the focus of Polish aid on democracy assistance to its Eastern neighbours should be interpreted as a backlash against Russian influence and argued that Poland's recent past has been its "asset and a responsibility" (Curry,

46 *Galia Chimiak and Katarzyna Zalas-Kamińska*

2010: 42). In 2015 the then vice foreign minister Konrad Pawlik likewise defended the decision to focus on supporting the transformation processes in Eastern Partnership countries. Polish aid professionals engaged in developmental CSOs also voiced the same conviction, i.e. that the country's focus on transferring its transformation know-how is an asset and a responsibility of Polish aid. It should be pointed out here that the geographic focus of Polish aid is a continuity of the engagement of Polish developmental CSOs in the region. Before Poland joined the EU in 2004, almost all Polish CSOs, which primary field of activity was international cooperation, focused on Ukraine.

This is not to imply that the sub-sector of Polish internationalised CSOs has always been unanimous when it came to the priorities of their work abroad. Discrepancies became evident when representatives of democratising and developmental CSOs came to work together in the umbrella organisation *Grupa Zagranica*. One aid professional even opined that *"Rightist fringes opt for working in the East... [whereas] Africa attracts the leftist fringes"*. Participation in working groups in *Grupa Zagranica* helped diminish these differences though.

As one respondent explained, *"This division... ... used to be more noticeable. We have begun to understand that we are one sector. In any way, this breach is rather a geographical one"*. What more, CSOs working in development came to realise that elements of democratisation and investing in local ownership are indispensable for the long-term success of any development intervention. Aid professionals from Polish CSOs provided further arguments for the focus on democratisation:

> "When we joined the EU, we were encouraged to support the former French colonies. We have no such obligation... . Central Asian countries are as poor as African ones" but also opined that "our [Polish] advantage is that most of our consultants speak Russian". Another CSO practitioner argued "We have this advantage that ... we [now] are the affluent West. On the other hand, we still belong to the rest of the world; as far as our mentality goes, we are closer to the people of Myanmar, than to the Dutch".

The ultimate explanation for Polish CSOs' focus on democratisation is however explained in the following: *"it is not so much a matter of having some concrete transformation experiences to share... but the credibility of Polish CSOs, when they work with partners from Ukraine or Georgia"*. Another aid professional spoke in a similar manner: *"We [in Poland] have a similar experience with a totalitarian system. And we have successfully got out of this system. ... Poland stands for an example that one can [do it], and it is worthwhile to take this road [to self-determination]"*.

Being at the forefront 47

Those aid professional who believed that the trademark of Poland in development cooperation is the country's experience with peaceful transformation, were clear about specifying their understanding of democratisation and development. As one of them explained, "*Poland does not believe in development without empowerment... .... I say empowerment, not liberal democracy*". A representative of a CSO implementing projects in post-Soviet Asian states argued that

"In Asia we are better off, because we understand the cultural specificity of these countries. We are capable of not imposing democratisation and participation [as it is understood in the West], but identify the existing mechanism on the spot... and involve the local leaders [to own the project], because this is how these communities have been functioning for thousands of years".

The discussion whether democratisation or development could be the comparative advantage of Polish aid reflects a wider cleavage on the competing notions of Polish public diplomacy, where "modernity fights with tradition; a pro-European stance with a national-conservative position" (Ociepka, 2013: 52). Indeed, the choice of partner countries of Polish internationalised CSOs' has impacted more than the targeted communities. The seminal role played by CSOs in both creating public awareness about development-related issues and advocating for greater involvement in development cooperation at political level has been highlighted (Lightfoot & Zubizarreta, 2011: 178). CSOs' engagement in public diplomacy and global education has been crucial in achieving these aims.

Polish CSOs' role in public diplomacy

Since its accession to NATO and the EU, Poland has been striving to redefine its desired international position into regional medium-sized power in European politics. According to Ryszard Zięba one of the expected internationals roles for Poland was transferring its model of successful democracy transformation to other countries (Zięba, 2010: 68). At the same time, for Poland, as for other post-communist members of the EU, geopolitics became an important element of public diplomacy strategy. Therefore Poland naturally took a position of promoting democracy eastwards, especially in relation to Belarus and Ukraine. Development cooperation, including support for democratisation in the east, was supposed to support the implementation of public diplomacy tasks (MSZ, 2013:5).

Many Polish internationalised CSOs engaged in development cooperation and democratisation assistance got to be involved in public

48 Galia Chimiak and Katarzyna Zalas-Kamińska

diplomacy efforts, even though these initiatives were not originally defined as public diplomacy. In the initial period of CSOs' foreign activity, these undertakings were referred to as *social diplomacy* and emphasised mainly how supporting democratic changes in other countries builds a positive image of Poland (MSZ, 2002; MSZ, 2004; Czubek, 2002: 3, 11). In Polish strategic documents CSOs were also appreciated for their efforts for the development of civil societies to the east of Poland (MSZ, 2006: 19-24). According to Janusz Kowalczyk, this approach was particularly pronounced in the case of Poland's policy towards Ukraine: both the contacts and cooperation between Polish and Ukrainians civil societies constituted a significant supplement to the political cooperation that has been developing since 1990s (Kowalczyk, 2013: 349). What's more, Poles were to contribute to a greater understanding for Ukrainian needs among Western countries (Stemplowski, 2007: 317).

As soon as public diplomacy[3] was officially introduced to Polish foreign policy tasks in 2008/2009, CSOs – among other public entities such as Polish diplomatic missions and Polish institutes abroad – were described as "highly valued partners" (MSZ, 2011: 22). The cooperation with the Polish CSOs in development aid was recognised as an increasingly significant element of Polish public diplomacy (MSZ: 2011: 3; MSZ, 2012: 22). Polish CSOs were contributors to Polish public diplomacy in the following areas: Polish transformation experience (know-how in successful transformation, democracy promotion); messages on Polish recent history, including its key events; counteracting the negative image of Poland, including promotion of Polish historical memory; celebrating famous Poles' years (the Janusz Korczak Year and the Year of Bruno Schulz, 2012), organising debates on the future of the EU, or debates on Polish-Jewish dialogue. Polish CSOs were responsible for projects implementation, including study visits to Poland and scholarship programs, but also for tourism, culture and entrepreneurship promotion. Many of these initiatives focused on the Eastern Partnership countries, mainly on Belarus and Ukraine (Zalas-Kamińska, 2019: 100-129, 189-192).

When it comes to project implementation, "partnership approach and cooperation among equals", "respect for diversity", "showing the direction", "passing on experiences instead of lecturing and giving ready-made instructions", "mutual learning", as well as "understanding and patience", were mentioned as distinctive characteristics of Polish CSOs by recipients of Polish activities (Zalas-Kamińska 2019: 130-134). Bartosz Sobotka claimed that good cooperation between Polish CSOs and their eastern neighbours resulted from their cultural affiliation. Historical similarities – in terms of Slavic ethnicity and affiliated languages – between Poles, Ukrainians and Belarusians constitute "a natural space for mutual understanding, which is missing in contacts with western European cultures representatives" (Sobotka, 2012: 91–92).

Being at the forefront 49

Indeed, Poland turned out to be close to these nations in terms of its social proximity and to the memory of the post-1989 changes, which was seen as a possible trajectory to be implemented in other eastern countries, if not by the present, then by the future generations (Zalas-Kamińska, 2019: 182–183).

Above all, CSOs activity was about building countless social relations. Primarily, Polish CSOs initiatives meant establishing mutual direct contacts between various stakeholders, including social activists, journalists, civil servants. The discourse between attachment to Christian values, history and tradition and aspiration for European integration and modernisation, values related to freedom and human rights, which were described as dominating in Poland after 1989, could paradoxically contribute to a better understanding of eastern societies on the path of change. Poland's eastern neighbours were provided with a perspective of preserving their culture and tradition, while experiencing the value of democracy and western integration; something that was described as "achieving smooth successful transformation without losing national traditions" (Zalas-Kamińska, 2019: 183). As it was pointed out by Krzysztof Stanowski:

> "...public diplomacy is about making people targeted by our programs feel that we are nor mercenaries, that no one has paid us for our activities. We share a piece of our own life: Poland is an example of the country that has undergone a successful transformation. The people of these countries know that success with no bloodshed involved is possible, because this is what we managed to do"
> (Nocuń, 2013: 31).

Although CSOs representatives were not, by definition, Polish transformation ambassadors, they somehow, and through their actions, became "allies of democracy". Within their actions, Poland, and more broadly, the western world and its values, were – at least partly – perceived through the prism of these particular people. Moreover, for many eastern partner countries' beneficiaries of cooperation projects, the arrival to Poland was their first foreign trip to the west. On the one hand, Warsaw has become a symbol of successful transformation, yet one where traditional values have been preserved; on the other hand, Poland stood for the West associated with respect for human rights and freedom, higher standard of living and many development opportunities. The transformation in Poland proved that change is possible.

Limitations and fields for future research

The presented above empirical studies' limitations have to do with the fact that they were conducted just before the change of political climate

50 *Galia Chimiak and Katarzyna Zalas-Kamińska*

in the country. Since 2015, the coalition government led by the Law and Justice party has enhanced its financial support to "conservative" CSOs while cutting funding for organisations reportedly treated previously favourably by state and private donors. A study of watchdog CSOs' reaction to the new legal environment has found that, unlike Hungary, where specific CSOs have been targeted, in Poland the focus has been on "dividing the civil society and marginalising the CSOs which were not in favour of the government" (Szuleka, 2018: 18). The resulting cleavage in the Polish civil society sector should be understood in light of the turn towards illiberal democratic practices where "dissenters are typically regarded as existential enemies in a zero-sum political game" (Krawatzek & Soroka, 2021: 16). This process has been called "pillarisation" and is understood as the "vertical segregation of civil society into distinct compartments with limited interaction across a dividing boundary (be it religious, ethnic, political)" (Ekiert, 2020: 9). Clearly, future research – in Poland as well as in other countries where cultural polarisation was reinforced by populist tendencies in politics – needs to focus on the impact of this new reality on the functioning of CSOs engaged in development cooperation and public diplomacy alike. It should be expected that Polish CSOs contribution to development cooperation, democracy assistance and public diplomacy efforts will be continued. With its experience, the CSO sector is not only prompt to implement projects, but also to educate, raise awareness, initiate "dialogue in the country and abroad" and serve "as a watchdog for governmental efforts" (Ociepka, 2017: 160). Special consideration will have to be given to the growing CSOs capacity in terms of obtaining funds for their activities from non-public sources.

Conclusions

Undoubtedly, Polish civil society's experiences in the 1980s and the 1990s made them become a natural asset of Polish eastern specialisation, especially in terms of Poland's support for its eastern neighbours' civil societies' development (Zdanowicz & Doliwa-Klepacka, 2010: 165-182). Thus, in accordance with constructivist theorising, Polish CSOs engaged in public diplomacy and development cooperation did act as "policy entrepreneurs" (Adler, 2008: 104). Polish CSOs intuitively grasped the specificity of societies in partner countries, and supported them without exposing the projects to misunderstanding of the action's context. Polish CSOs' engagement's distinctive characteristic was their civil character and a high level of socialisation (Stanowski, 2013). Their ability to extend western-eastern mutual understanding by employing their first-hand transformation experience and bring respect for diversity constituted the comparative advantage of Polish CSOs over entities from established donor countries.

Being at the forefront 51

It is said that there has been a natural change of generation within Polish CSOs, where people involved in the democratic opposition and those who have experienced first-hand the Polish transformation and democracy building process no longer constitute the majority of aid professionals. However, the legacy left by them within thriving organisations led by professionals imbued with democratic values, allows to believe that these unique experiences will not be wasted. Polish citizens' and CSOs' authentic support for Euromaidan, later on in response to the migration crisis at the Polish-Belarusian border, and most recently at the Ukrainian border when Russian aggression started in February 24, 2022, corroborate this observation. CSOs' determination to act made them active faster than any state (OkOpress, 2022). What's more, they have continued their support, regardless of political decisions made at various levels. Individual Polish citizens likewise demonstrated strong support for Ukrainian refugees fleeing their war-torn country (CBOS, 2022). The cost of refugees' living expenses in Poland, within bilateral ODA, are estimated to have grown by more than 50% compared to the previous year, i.e. before the war in Ukraine. Even though the inclusion of this type of expenses in ODA is justifiably criticised by the European CSOs community (Sharples, 2021: 27), the decision itself to provide refugees with this support needs to be assessed positively. The 2022 perspectives indicates that these expenditures, and therefore this commitment, will be highest among OECD countries (NFP, 2022).

As public diplomacy has become "less national", and more collaborative (Melissen, 2015: 450), CSOs efforts for transferring democratisation is a challenge for states' foreign policies, including Poland and its eastern specialisation. It is especially relevant nowadays when the Western world has to face issues such as the rise of illiberal democracy, the growing influence of "conservative, nationalistic, anti-liberal" networks (Ekiert, 2020: 12), as well as right-wing "mega-donors" and "pseudo-Catholic, far-right mobilisation" (Datta, 2021) on national affairs in Poland and beyond. CSOs promoting human rights and espousing democratic values have proved valuable and indispensable stakeholders in public diplomacy and development cooperation alike. They need both recognition and ongoing support in order to be able to perform their critically important function in the democratic state.

Notes

1 On September 14, 2022, the European Commission's chief Ursula von der Leyen admitted, "We should have listened to the voices inside our Union — in Poland, in the Baltics, and all across Central and Eastern Europe. They have been telling us for years that Putin would not stop.", see https://www.politico. eu/article/von-der-leyens-russia-mea-culpa-gets-kremlinology-treatment/

52 *Galia Chimiak and Katarzyna Zalas-Kamińska*

2 Quotations in this sub-chapter come from an empirical study conducted among Polish aid professionals and analysed in detail in G. Chimiak. (2006). The Growth of Non-governmental Development Organisations in Poland and Their Cooperation with Polish Aid, IFiS Publisher.

3 According to the MFA, public diplomacy is aimed at shaping social attitudes and public opinion abroad, gaining understanding and support for the Polish raison d'état and Polish foreign policy; it uses soft power mechanism (the promotion of Polish culture, history, science, language, education, spot, tourism, economics) to build positive image of Poland; its activities are aimed at foreign institutions and organisations and societies (MSZ, 2009).

References

Adler, E. (2008). Constructivism and International Relations. In: W. Carlsnaes, Th. Risse, B.A Simmons (Eds.), *Handbook of International Relations.* SAGE, 95–118.

Broś, N. (2017). Public diplomacy and cooperation with non-governmental organizations in the liberal perspective of international relations. *Journal of Education Culture and Society*, no. 1, 11–21.

CBOS. (2022) Jak Polacy pomagają uchodźcom z Ukrainy?. CBOS Newsletter 14/ 2022. https://www.cbos.pl/PL/publikacje/news/newsletter_ver3.php?news_r= 2022&news_nr=14

Chimiak, G. (2016). *The Growth of Non-governmental Development Organisations in Poland and Their Cooperation with Polish Aid.* IFiS Publisher.

Cooper, A.F., Heine, J., Thakur, R. (2015). Introduction In: A. F. Cooper, J. Heine, R. Thakur (Eds.) *The Oxford Handbook of Modern Diplomacy.* Oxford University Press.

Curry, A. (2010). Poland's New Ambitions. *Wilson Quarterly*, no 34/2, 38–42.

Czubek, Gr. (2002). *Social Diplomacy. The Case of Poland. International activity of Polish NGOs and Their Dialogue with Government.* Fundacja Stefana Batorego.

Datta, N. (2021). *Tip of the Iceberg: Religious Extremist Funders against Human Rights for Sexuality and Reproductive Health in Europe 2009–2018.* European Parliamentary Forum for Sexual & Reproductive Rights

Drążkiewicz, E. (2020). *Institutionalized Dreams: The Art of Managing Foreign Aid,* Berghahn Books.

Ekiert, G. (2020). Civil Society as a Threat to Democracy: Organizational Bases for the Populist Counterrevolution in Poland. Centre for European Studies Harvard. https://issuu.com/ces.harvard/docs/ekiert_working_paper_-_2020_-_final.

Gruca, G. (2011). History and Challenges of Polish Aid: The Polish Humanitarian Action Case. In K. Pędziwiatr et al. (Eds.) *Current Challenges to Peacebuilding Efforts and Development Assistance.* Tischner European University.

Hochstetler, K. (2015). Civil Society. In: A.F. Cooper et al. (eds.), *The Oxford Handbook of Modern Diplomacy.* Oxford University Press.

Isar, Y. R. (2022). Civil Society Actors in International Cultural Diplomacy. In: M. Hoelscher, R. A. List, A. Ruser, S. Toepler (eds), *Civil Society: Concepts, Challenges, Contexts. Nonprofit and Civil Society Studies.* Springer. 10.1007/ 978-3-030-98008-5_16

Jasikowska, K. (2018). *Zmieniając świat. Edukacja globalna między zyskiem a zbawieniem.* Impuls.

Being at the forefront 53

Kopiński, D. (2012). Visegrád Countries' Development Aid to Africa: Beyond the Rhetoric. *Perspectives on European Politics and Society*, 13, 33–49.

Kowalczyk, J. (2013). Miejsce i rola "dyplomacji społecznej" w polityce Polski wobec Ukrainy In: B. Surmacz, *Nowe oblicza dyplomacji*. Wydawnictwo UMCS.

Krawatzek, F. and Soroka, G. (2021). Circulation, conditions, claims: examining the politics of historical memory in Eastern Europe. *East European Politics and Societies*. 10.1177/0888325420969786

Lightfoot, S. (2010). The Europeanisation of International Development Policies: The Case of Central and Eastern European States. *Europe-Asia Studies*, 62, 329–350.

Lightfoot, S. and Lindenhovius Zubizarreta, I. (2011). The Emergence of International Development Policies in Central and Eastern European States. In: P. Hoebink (Ed.), *European Development Cooperation: In between the Local and the Global*. Amsterdam University Press.

Martens, K. (2002). Mission Impossible? Defining Nongovernmental Organisations. *Voluntas*, 13, 271–285.

Melissen, J. (2015). Public Diplomacy. In A.F. Cooper, J. Heine, R. Thakur (eds.), *The Oxford Handbook of Modern Diplomacy*. Oxford: Oxford University Press.

MSZ. (2002). *Informacja ministra spraw zagranicznych Włodzimierza Cimoszewicza o podstawowych kierunkach polityki zagranicznej Polski* 14.03.2002.

MSZ. (2004). *Informacja ministra spraw zagranicznych Włodzimierza Cimoszewicza o zadaniach polskiej polityki zagranicznej w 20024 roku*, 21.01.2014.

MSZ. (2006). *Polska współpraca na rzecz rozwoju. Raport roczny 2006*.

MSZ. (2009). *Kierunki promocji Polski do 2015 r Dokument przyjęty przez Radę Promocji Polski w 2009*.

MSZ. (2011). *Polska współpraca na rzecz rozwoju. Raport roczny 2010*.

MSZ. (2012). *Dyplomacja publiczna 2011*.

MSZ. (2013). *Dyplomacja publiczna 2012*.

Nocuń, M. (2013). Krowa a sprawa polska In: M. Nocuń, M. Żyła, Sektor mocy. Polska się liczy, *Tygodnik Powszechny*, 30/3342.

Nye, J. (2004). *Soft Power: The Means to Success in World Politics*. Public Affairs.

Notes from Poland. (2022). Poland to spend €8.4bn supporting Ukraine refugees in 2022, highest in OECD, https://notesfrompoland.com/2022/10/14/poland-to-spend-e8-4bn-supporting-ukraine-refugees-in-2022-highest-in-oecd/?fbclid=IwAR1bZQ7iWTPrVlsBWXy33zsrZGz5gn_5puWxnVW5JsWgbyrM0pN0hfo dFZ0, accessed: 19.10.2022

Ociepka, B. (2013). New Members' Public Diplomacy. In M.K. Davis and J. Melissen. (Eds.) *European Public Diplomacy. Soft Power at Work*. Palgrave Macmillan, 39–56.

Ociepka, B. (2017). *Poland's new ways of public diplomacy*. Peter Lang.

OKOpress, (2022), *137 polskich organizacji pozarządowych wspólnie apeluje o solidarność z Ukrainą*, 22.02.2022, https://oko.press/137-polskich-organizacji-pozarzadowych-wspolnie-apeluje-o-solidarnosc-z-ukraina-to-nasza-sprawa/, access: 05.08.2022.

Pamment, J. (2016). *Intersections between Public Diplomacy & International Development. Case Studies in Converging Fields*. Figueroa Press.

54   Galia Chimiak and Katarzyna Zalas-Kamińska

Pisarska, K. (2008). The role of the new Member States in the developing of the EU's Eastern agenda in the years 2004-2007 – perceptions of EU officials. *Pulaski Report 1/2008* (accessed 19.06.2015 at http://pulaski.pl/images/publikacje/raport/Pulaski_Report_No_1_08_English.pdf).

Pospieszna, P. (2014). *Democracy Assistance from the Third Wave: Polish Engagement in Belarus and Ukraine.* University of Pittsburg Press.

Schmitz, H. P. & Sikkink, K. (2008). International Human Rights. In:W. Carlsnaes, Th. Risse & B.A.

Sharples, A. (2021), *AID WATCH 2021. A Geopolitical Commission: Building Partnership or Playing Politics,* CONCORD, (accesses 19.10.2022 at https://aidwatch.concordeurope.org/2021-report/) Simmons (Eds.). *Handbook of International Relations.* SAGE, 517-537.

Sobotka, B. (2012). *Tworzenie polskiego systemu pomocy rozwojowej.* CeDeWu.

Stanowski, K. (2002). Z kart historii współpracy polskich organizacji pozarządowych w III RP z partnerami społecznymi. In: G. Czubek (Ed.) *Międzynarodowa działalność polskich organizacji pozarządowych.* Fundacja Stefana Batorego.

Stanowski, K. (2013). *Demokracja – polski produkt eksportowy,* 10.07.2013, Instytut Obywatelski (accessed 10.01.2015 at http://www.instytutobywatelski.pl/16038/komentarze/demokracja-polski-produkt-eksportowy).

Stemplowski, R. (2007). *Wprowadzenie do analizy polityki zagranicznej.* PISM.

Surmacz B. (2014). Dyplomacja organizacji pozarządowych. *Stosunki Międzynarodowe – International Relations,* 1/19, 51–70.

Sussman, G. (2010). *Branding Democracy. U.S. Regime Change in Post-Soviet Eastern Europe.* Peter Lang Publishing.

Szuleka, M. (2018). First victims or last guardians? The consequences of rule of law backsliding for NGOs: case studies of Hungary and Poland. CEPS Paper in Liberty and Security in Europe No. 2018-06. https://www.ceps.eu/system/files/MSzuleka_RoLandNGOs.pdf

Wróbel, A. (2003). Wspólne problemy, wspólne działania. In *Polska--Ukraina. Współpraca organizacji pozarządowych.* Fundacja im. Stefana Batorego, 16–24.

Zaharna, R.S. (2009). Mapping out a Spectrum of Public Diplomacy Initiatives. Informational and Relational Communication Frameworks. In N. Snow, P. M. Taylor (Eds.), *Routledge Handbook of Public Diplomacy.* Routledge.

Zalas-Kamińska, K. (2019). *Poles in Aid. Polskie organizacje pozarządowe w pomocy rozwojowej a dyplomacja publiczna.* Księgarnia Akademicka.

Zatepilina-Monacell, O. (2012). High Stakes: U.S. Nonprofit Organizations and the U.S. Standing Abroad. *Public Relations Review,* 38, 471–476.

Zdanowicz, M., Doliwa-Klepacka A. (2010). Społeczeństwo obywatelskie w autorytarnych państwach postradzieckich objętych Partnerstwem Wschodnim In: M. Zdanowicz, T. Dubowski, A. Piekutowska *Partnerstwo Wschodnie. Wymiary realnej integracji.* Uniwersytet w Białymstoku.

Zięba, R. (2010). Poszukiwanie międzynarodowej roli dla Polski – konceptualizacja roli państwa "średniej rangi" In: S. Bieleń (ed.), *Polityka zagraniczna Polski po wstąpieniu do NATO i Unii Europejskiej: Problemy adaptacji i tożsamości.* Difin.

6 Barriers to CSOs' public diplomacy

Failure of multilateral intervention, conflict, violence and militarism

Ibrahim Natil

Introduction

To understand the Middle East Quartet's multilateralism, it is essential to examine the theory of John Ruggie who describes 'multilateralism is an institutional form which coordinates relations among three or more states on the basis of "generalised" principles of conduct … without regard to the particularistic interests of the parties or the strategic exigencies that may exist in any specific occurrence' (Ruggie, 1992: 571). The Quartet is a group of nations and international and supranational entities as (Bouchard & Peterson, 2010) writes 'three or more actors engaging in more or less institutionalised and voluntary cooperation governed by norms or rules that apply more or less equally to all'.

The Quartet has faced a number of challenges since its early days of formal engagement in the conflict. The Middle East Quartet is considered an advanced cooperation of multilateralism to assist both Palestine and Israel to reach a compromise. The Quartet comprises the United Nations, the European Union, the United States and Russia, which were set up in Madrid in 2002, recalling Madrid Conference of 1991, as a result of the escalating conflict between the Palestinians and the Israelis. The Quartet describes its own mandate as 'to help mediate Middle East peace negotiations and to support Palestinian economic development and institution-building in preparation for eventual statehood'. The Quartet compromises of the United Nations, the European Union, the United States and Russia to assist the Israelis and Palestinians to implement a two states solution. It is a multilateral track approach to end the violence and involve both parties in peace talks. It is sometimes called Quartet on the Middle East or Middle East Quartet or the Diplomatic Quartet or Madrid Quartet or simply the Quartet. It is a 'coordinated mechanism' to engage in Palestine/Israel conflict.

DOI: 10.4324/9781003441465-6

56 *Ibrahim Natil*

Quartet, however, is not a new concept of multilateralism, but there was an early example of multilateralism when the great powers of nineteenth-century Europe coordinated their management of the international system by moderating their own behaviour and consulting with one another over any territorial changes. Tocci (2013) writes 'EU has been the principal driver behind the Quartet as Morningstar (2004) emphasises on the multilateralism approach of Europe 'Europe does emphasise multilateralism'. Through the Quartet, the EU sought to promote 'effective multilateral' cooperation and intervention in the Middle East conflict based on 'indivisibility', 'indiscrimination' and 'reciprocity' where all *members* are equal participants in the cooperative attempt through 'cooperated mechanism' according to the Quartet's mandate and scope of work. The Quartet's representatives of EU, UN, USA and Russia communicate and meet regularly at the high level (Quartet Website, 2018).

The Quartet represents a case of 'crystallising multilateralism' as is seen as valuable not only because it supports cooperated mechanism and prevents political rivalries while they communicate and meet regularly at the level of the Quartet Principals. Multilateralism still provides entities with many advantages, it raises challenges as well. This is particularly true when entities with differing levels of power coordinate their behaviour. Richard Morningstar (2004), however, writes, 'the United States does often act more unilaterally than other nations, and Europe does emphasise multilateralism. Yet neither has a monopoly on one paradigm or the other'. Through this engagement with the Quartet, the USA administration, during the second term of President George Bush, sought a diplomatic cover and international legitimacy provided by UN approval to advance its own individual interests and goals in such places as Iraq, Iran and North Korea. Tocci, (2011) discussed 'the Quartet was applauded by many at the time as an effective multilateralisation of Middle East mediation'.

Richard Morningstar (2004) writes, however, 'the United States need not subject itself to the dictates of any international organizations because in our "exceptionalist" view, we do things correctly'. This refers to rule-governed behaviour in which the Quartet's members keep their pursuit of immediate goals, to achieve their own long-run values and interests through cooperation with Palestinians and Israelis. To understand the challenges facing the Quartet, owing to influence of the USA's unilateralist approach in Palestine/Israel conflict after President Trump's proclamation on Jerusalem and aid cut to the Palestinian institutions and refugees including UNRWA (Independent, 2018).

Methodology

The author analyses and reviews the relevant literature to understand the objectives and scope of work as multilateral track of the Middle East

Barriers to CSOs' public diplomacy 57

Quartet. The author also interviewed some civil society activists and used observation and interaction with activists and specialists to enrich debate about the Quartet's contribution to resolving the Middle East conflict between the Israelis and the Palestinians. The author also discusses if the Quartet has been neutral and efficient in its own attempts to end violence and contribute to peace in the regional from Palestinian perspective. This aims at examining if the USA's unilateral decisions had already challenged and influenced the Quartet's 'coordinated mechanism'. This chapter, however, critically analyses the USA's unilateralist approach after 'Trump's deal' or the 'deal of the century', the relocations of its embassy to Jerusalem and cutting aid to the Palestinian institutions and *UNRWA* and their impact on the future of Palestine/Israel conflict. The author also examines the implications of these changes on the principles and the fundamental values of the Quartet as multilateral forum to reduce the spread and escalation of violent conflict in the Palestinian Occupied Territories -OPT and its impact on the civil society.

This chapter critically analyses the USA's unilateralist approach after 'Trump's deal' or the 'deal of the century', the relocations of its embassy to Jerusalem and aid cuts to Palestinian civil society organisations (CSOs) and *UNRWA* and their impact on the future of Palestine/Israel conflict. Therefore, it is essential to investigate the Quartet's qualitative dimension, efficiency and engagement in accordance with its mandate as a formal multilateral forum. It also examines, however, the barriers to Biden's administration which have failed in reverting Trump's administration's political decisions, for example, reopening the US Consulate in Jerusalem and PLO office in Washington, despite the fact of his July 2022 trip to the region. Biden's trip to the Middle East indicates the fierce competition among the great powers of the USA, Russia and China. The US would not leave the Middle East to its competitors as the war on Ukraine indicates the importance of the Middle East geopolitical location, which enjoys huge reserves of oil, gas and energy resources.

Quartet engagement

On October 25, 2001, a multilateral initiative began to take a place in international politics as representatives of the EU, UN and the US and Russian governments met the former Palestinian leader, Yasser Arafat to conclude a cease-fire and to endorse his policy of implementing security reforms in the Palestinian Authority (PA), following the outbreak of the second armed uprising in September 2000. During this time, the initiative was only an informal multilateral cooperation without a formal structure. Charles Lipson (1991) has argued that the flexibility and low political profile of 'informal cooperation' may sometimes make this a preferable means of acting multilaterally. However, a former

58 *Ibrahim Natil*

Palestinian diplomate said 'the Palestinian President, Yasser Arafat, found this initiative an opportunity to increase the international multilateral track and Russia's engagement in the peace process after the USA's failure to break a deal between the Palestinians and Israelis at the Camp David negotiations in summer 2000'.

However, multilateral informal cooperation was still inefficient without active and direct engagement to end violence between the Israelis and the Palestinians since the failure of the 'peace process'. In April 2002, the same representatives agreed to transform their cooperation into a formal structure. The 'Quartet' as a follow-up of the Israeli-Palestinian peace process, called again for the implementation of a ceasefire agreement brokered by the US administration (Tocci, 2011). The Quartet was established while the Israeli forces were conducting its massive military operation, 'Defensive Shield', in the Palestinian areas, which destroyed the PA's institutions, some civil society organisations and besieged the Palestinian leader, Yasser Arafat, in his office in the West Bank City of Ramallah (Natil, 2015). However, the efficiency, legitimacy and power of such forums and structures to achieve their goals were introduced by Kenneth Abbot and Duncan Snidal (1998). Therefore, it is essential to discuss the efficiency of the Quartet's engagement as a formal multilateral forum in accordance with its own objectives and scope of work as follows:

Institutional Reforms

The Quartet's representatives had already cooperated with the Israelis and key influential members from the PA to put tremendous pressure on the former Palestinian leader, Yasser Arafat, to accept the 'Road Map' plan, brokered by the US administration. The Quartet endorsed the 'Road Map' plan to introduce a number of institutional reforms to limit Arafat's power and his control over the PA's security and financial institutions (Elgindy, 2012). The PA's responded to the Quartet's conditions and introduced a new structure and hired an empowered prime minister who would lead new arrangements to end the 'second uprising'. The new structure also included the appointment of a new minister of security and a new minister of finance. Dr Salam Fayed, a former World Bank staff member who was out of the PA's elite circle had been appointed by the PA in 2003. His appointment was a condition by the Quartet's members to continue channelling the foreign aid to the PA. A serious part of the Quartet's conditions, the PA reformed and restructured its security agency while a special USA security expert was involved in training its officers and watching the PA's commitments to the Quartet's conditions.

Biden reiterated on his joint speech with the Palestinian President, the word 'reforms', which the Palestinian Authority (PA) should introduce.

Barriers to CSOs' public diplomacy 59

This repeated magic word reflects the complexities of the political landscape, of which the USA has been unable to progress towards the direction of peace. The subsequent US administration shows its power to manage the conflict, not solve it despite various cycles of violence since the Oslo declarations in September 1993.

End violence and political deadlock

The Quartet was mainly established to assist the Palestinians to end the second uprising after the failure of the peace process with the Israelis. The Quartet's envoy from its members involved in dialogue and formal diplomacy with Palestinians and the Israelis to end violence. The USA took the lead to mediate a cease-fire, supported by the Quartet, Egypt and Jordan based on the 'Road Map' plan. In 2003, the USA also engaged with the first Prime Minister, Mahmud Abbas (the current president), who succeeded in persuading the various factions including Hamas and Islamic Jihad to give his government a chance to respect the cease-fire reached between the PA and Israel on June 29, 2003. The cease-fire, however, failed in less than 100 days when a member of Hamas' military wing from Hebron did not adhere to Hamas' leadership's instructions, and carried out a suicide bombing in Western Jerusalem, killing twenty-one Israelis on August 19, 2003 (International Crisis Group, 2004).

The USA and the Quartet engaged with other Palestinian politicians while the Palestinian leader, Yasser Arafat was still isolated and confined in his compound by the Israeli forces. However, Shlomo Ben Ami, a former foreign minister of Israel, writes of Arafat's passing from the political scene on November 11, 2004 as a tragedy because he was 'the only man whose signature on an agreement of compromise and reconciliation, which would include giving up unattainable dreams, could have been legitimate in the eyes of his people' (Ben-Ami, 2006: 324). After Arafat, the Quartet also endorsed the Israeli unilateral 'disengagement plan' from the Gaza Strip, implemented fully on September 12, 2005. Supporting unilateral disengagement from Gaza Strip without a future plan killed the peace process as (Siegman, 2006) writes:

It was killed—with malice aforethought—by Sharon's "unilateralism" with which he implemented the disengagement from Gaza, which in turn provided cover for his continued unilateralism. That he was bringing off the disengagement against the wishes of the settlers helped to divert attention from his refusal to have any negotiations with the Palestinians. Unilateralism continues to serve as the euphemism for Israeli policies that are expropriating half of what was to have been the state of Palestine, and are concentrating the Palestinian population, about to outnumber the Jewish population, in territorially disconnected

60   *Ibrahim Natil*

Bantustans that make a mockery of the promise of an independent, sovereign and viable Palestinian state made in the "road map" of 2003, which was put forward by the Quartet of the US, the EU, the UN, and Russia.

The Israeli government unilateral decision to 'disengage' with the Gaza Strip left it isolated and a subject to Israeli blockade, and frequent military operations. In the summer of 2014, for example, Israeli forces conducted 51 days of a military operation which already created a new environment of destruction, overloaded with psychological problems. It left 100,000 Gazans homeless and over 2,100 Gazans dead, the majority of them Palestinian civilians, compared with 76 Israeli fatalities, all soldiers (Natil, 2014: 82–87). The Quartet involved in and led the boycotting of the Hamas government that was elected in 2006, by imposing three conditions on Hamas: unless it agreed to renounce violence, recognise Israel and abide by previous agreements between PLO and Israel. Russia, a member of the Quartet, however, engaged in dialogue with Hamas shortly after the Quartet boycotted the Hamas government. Russia invited Khalid Mishael to visit Moscow for a meeting on March 3, 2006. The Russian government explained publicly that its intention was to persuade Hamas to change its political position with regard to Israel and the peace process. Some saw this initiative as evidence of Russia's attempt to use the Palestinian issue to regain a foothold in the Middle East, which Russia had lost after the collapse of the Soviet Union (Natil, 2015:97).

This invitation was an unexpected step, as Hamas was still listed as a terrorist organisation by the USA and by the EU, and Russia was a member of the Middle East Quartet. This contradicted the multilateral concept, introduced by (Ruggie, 1992: 571) 'without particularistic interests of the parties or the strategic exigencies that may exist in any specific occurrence' and emphasised unilateral interest of each member. This reflected a visible division and unilateralist approach that had already undermined the 'cooperated mechanism' of the Quartet itself. Tony Blair, however, held at least six lengthy private meetings with former Hamas political bureau chief, Khaled Meshaal after he had left the Quartet to explore a possible long-term cease-fire between Israel and Hamas. 'We were wrong to boycott Hamas after its election win' Blair said on October 14, 2017. Blair experienced earlier inefficiency of Quartet's as Saban Centre for Middle East Policy reported in 2012:

> The current mechanism is too outdated, dysfunctional and discredited to be reformed. Instead of undertaking another vain attempt to 'reactivate' the Quartet, the United States, the European Union,

United Nations and Russia should simply allow the existing mechanism to go quietly into the night. The Quartet has little to show for its decade-long involvement in the peace process. Israelis and Palestinians are no closer to resolving the conflict, and in the few instances in which political negotiations did take place, the Quartet's role was usually relegated to that of a political bystander. Having spent most of the last three years in a state of near paralysis, and having failed to dissuade the Palestinians from seeking UN membership and recognition in September 2011, the Quartet has finally reached the limits of its utility (AlGindy, K., 2012).

The Quartet's conditions on Hamas and its dysfunctionality have already contributed to complicate the political, social and economic circumstances of the Gaza Strip, where Hamas has been isolated since 2006. The Quartet have failed to intervene to prevent a number of military attacks on the Gaza Strip, closure of civil society/human rights organisations and targeting and killing of journalists such as Shireen Abu Aqla on May 11, 2022, and continuous expansion of the Israeli settlements in the West Bank as (Natil, 2022) discusses.

The Quartet, however, kept urging the parties to take concrete steps to reunite Gaza and the West Bank under the PA's legitimacy and address the grave humanitarian situation in the Gaza Strip.

Economic Development

The Quartet's office in Jerusalem still addresses humanitarian issues and engages in economic mapping and the areas of energy, water, rule of law, movement and trade and telecommunication. The Quartet's staff still works in keeping its strategic principles: catalytic role, implementation of agreements reached and announcements made by the parties, bridging between the parties and providing creative solutions that enable progress on the ground. The staff also continues support to the Quartet envoys, including their work to enable greater Palestinian sovereignty over their own affairs and to realise a final status agreement. Its staff also engages in the complementarity of work with other key actors, including UNSCO, the Netherlands, Norway, the World Bank and the Local Aid Coordination Secretariat to support the PA's operations to develop its economy (Quartet's Office, 2018).

Foreign aid, however, has already dropped drastically during the last few years, owing to a number of reasons, including the absence of peace, the political and security challenges in the Middle East, in addition to the late global financial crisis and donors' priorities at home. However, Tony Blair, the Quartet's former envoy launched his own peace plan for the Israel-Palestine conflict, based on improving 'economic co-operation' in

62 *Ibrahim Natil*

May 2008. There had been, however, a number of Palestinian politicians and civil society leaders who criticised the Quartet's efficiency and its envoy, Tony Blair for failing to contribute to support economic development. In October 2011, Nabil Shaath, a senior adviser for Palestinian President Abbas accused Blair of talking 'like an Israeli diplomat'. Ghassan Khatib, vice-president of Birzeit University in the West Bank and a former Palestinian Authority cabinet minister said, 'I think it's the Quartet that failed to deliver. I think in general, Palestinians are disappointed by the performance of the Quartet. I cannot think of any serious thing that the Quartet succeeded to help us in' (Independent, 2012).

Since its set up, the Quartet has failed to introduce genuine changes to the peace process or economic improvement in the Occupied Palestinian Territories, while the image and neutrality of the US as the sole mediator for peace between Palestine and Israel has always been questioned after taking crucial unilateral decisions as Tocci (2011) writes:

> Its activities have reflected either the EU's unsuccessful attempts to frame American initiatives within a multilateral setting, or the US's successful attempts at providing a multilateral cover for unilateral actions. The Quartet is not without value. But to play a useful role, it should be enlarged and reshaped as a forum to establish a renewed international consensus on the Arab-Israeli conflict.

The Quartet did not succeed to assist the parties including key regional stakeholders to take an initiative to get actively engaged to improve the harsh economic and humanitarian circumstances of civil society in the Gaza Strip. It did not deliver practical solutions to end the deterioration of humanitarian security and circumstances in the Gaza Strip, however, its envoys only agreed, in its meeting in July 2013, to continue their regular engagement with Israelis and Palestinians, and key regional stakeholders (Quartet, July 2018). There has been, however, a series of challenges facing the Quartet since the arrival of President Trump at the White House in January 2017. The USA's administration had already changed the agreed rules or red lines since 1991, for a final status compromise between Palestinians and Israelis according to the Quartet's general principles. Richard Morningstar (2004) emphasises that 'the United States does often act more unilaterally than other nations.

Unilateral Action

On December 6, 2017, the Quartet's existence and the mandate was challenged by unilateral and unprecedented proclamation of the USA's president on Jerusalem as a capital for Israel. Palestinians from all social and political spectrums believed that Trump's decision was a full defiance of international law and all UN resolutions on Jerusalem. In 2015 and 2017, UNESCO announced that the old city of Jerusalem is Palestinian heritage sites. It also called on the 'occupying power' to end projects aimed at altering the *character and status of the Holy City*. They have a very strong spiritual connection and loyalty to the holy sites of Jerusalem. The Palestinians believe that Trump's Jerusalem proclamation assists Israel to create facts on the ground and to change the demographic and heritage structure as part of a plan to take full control of holy city. This supports Israeli plans, which are biblically driven and illegal actions according to frequent calls by UNESCO and the UN resolutions on Jerusalem.

In 1967, Israel annexed East Jerusalem and considered it as its own 'eternal' capital, which is not yet recognised internationally and is considered an occupied city according to international law. The Israelis commemorate every year their own control and sovereignty over Jerusalem after 3,000 years from the 'control of strangers' according to their biblical doctrine. Jerusalem also represents a core value for Palestinian identity and symbolism from religious and national perspectives as well. Mahmoud Abbas, the Palestinian President said that the Palestinians have been engaged with the President's advisors to achieve the 'deal of the century' but 'instead we got the slap of our times'. 'The United States has chosen to lose its qualification as a mediator ... We will no longer accept that it has a role in the political process' (Hawash, 2018). The PA's leadership was shocked from unexpected decision while waiting for Trump's 'ultimate deal', which considered it a 'political bribe' for Israel as Gershon Baskin writes:

'Trump's 'ultimate deal' is a primarily an Israeli/right-wing American plan with very strong influence from right-wing American Jews... American Jewish and Christian personalities swallowed with drunken pleasure the redesign of the Middle East with Palestine relegated to a semi-non-existence of some amorphous form of very limited autonomy under Israeli protection, which in reality is nothing but an unending Israeli occupation'

(Baskin, 2018).

This had already challenged the Quartet's mandate and its existence via his own unilateral decisions. The Quartet's members rejected Trump's unilateral decision but without any changes on the Quartet's current mechanism. Trump's predecessors have never attempted to change the USA's political position on Jerusalem prior to the final compromise or agreement between the Israelis and the Palestinians. This decision has already promoted the radical disagreement between the PA and the USA. The USA preferred to act unilaterally, exercising its own

64 *Ibrahim Natil*

'particularistic interests', against the Quartet's general principles and the classic concept of 'the multilateral cooperation', introduced by (Ruggie, 1992: 571). The USA also exercised its 'particularistic interests' to cut foreign aid to the Palestinian civil society institutions and UNRWA. Foreign aid had been a fundamental and essential instrument of U.S. foreign policy in Palestine/Israel 'peace process'.

Unilateralism and foreign aid

In January, 2018, Trump communicated his own anger at the Palestinians through Twitter 'we pay the Palestinians hundreds of millions of dollars a year and get no appreciation or respect'. With the Palestinians no longer willing to talk peace, why should we make any of these massive future payments to them? Historically, there has been sympathy with the Palestinians in the UN Assembly General, and the USA's previous administration never cut its contribution to UNRWA. In 2016, the US contributed $335 m to UNRWA and a similar sum was planned for 2018. President Trump's administration, however, wanted other countries to step up and contribute more after the PA suspended the political communications with Trump's administration (Independent, 2018). UNRWA represents the question of Palestinian refugees, which should be negotiated between the Palestinians and the Israelis in a final compromise. The USA planned to remove the question of refugees out of the negotiations table between the Palestinian and Israelis.

UNRWA is a relief and human development agency, established by the UN General Assembly in 1949, after many Palestinians fled or were expelled from their homes amidst the unrest following the establishment of the State of Israel. UNRWA delivers human development, relief and humanitarian services. UNRWA delivers these services to more than five million Palestinian refugees in the West Bank, Gaza Strip, Jordan, Syria and Lebanon. *UNRWA* is funded almost entirely by voluntary contributions from UN Member States. International donors including the USA, also assisted not only UNRWA but also many CSOs to continue playing a significant role in promoting processes of conflict resolution and human rights. Foreign aid to UNRWA and CSOs also aimed to support human rights, tolerance and conflict resolution programmes (Natil, 2016: 78–82).

UNRWA has been dealing with the most severe financial crisis since its establishment after the US dramatically reduced payment to UNRWA and assistance to Palestinians. UNRWA, however, was created with a remit to deliver services and assistance wherever refugees are located until their problem is solved. The US has been the largest donor responsible for nearly a third of the budget to UNRWA, which offers to assist the Palestinians refugees in its five areas of operation in the Middle East. However, the USA will donate to UNRWA $60 m in aid for

Barriers to CSOs' public diplomacy 65

Palestinians but will withhold another $65 m 'for future consideration' as White House spokesperson said (Independent, 2018).

Shortly, this cut had already left a very serious impact on already impoverished social and economic circumstances as UNRWA, for example, terminated the contracts of 400 engineers who worked for seven years in Gaza Strip. The local Palestinian CSOs also have already started to suffer from the aid cut (Srour, 2018). Generally, foreign aid is essential for programmes implementation and their effectiveness and impact (Lutz, M. Baliamoune-Lutz, 2016). This cut has increased the challenges of CSOs to respond to new massive challenges as they struggle to meet citizens' needs and demands efficiently, not least because resources are sorely lacking after years of blockades (Natil, 2014). Haneen Al Samak says 'aid cut will increase citizens' suffering and the pressures on the PA, and UNRWA, but the solidarity among various categories of the society may ease pressures for political causes and this may encourage the international community to get engaged once again' (Samak, 2018).

UNRWA had to launch a global campaign 'dignity is priceless', to increase international community engagement and Arab countries' contributions towards the financial crisis. UNRWA's campaign also will accept Zakat during Ramadan, while Muslim people always increase their donations and charity during this month. This cut had already altered a number of western and neighbouring countries as Sweden, Jordan and Egypt, which responded to this unprecedented and serious financial crisis of UNRWA, to take a global action and mobilisation in search for a solution to keep its operations. Sweden played a visible role by participating in co-chairing with Jordan and Egypt. Sweden led the international campaign, owing to its history of cooperation with UNRWA as Sweden's Minister for Foreign Affairs Margot Wallström says 'Sweden has a long history of close cooperation with UNRWA. In 2017, we were the Agency's fourth largest donor' (Government of Sweden, 2018).

On March 15, 2018, the extraordinary ministerial conference entitled, Preserving Dignity and Sharing Responsibility — Mobilizing Collective Action for UNRWA took place at the Food and Agriculture Organisation of the United Nations to mobilise both political and financial support for UNRWA. The organisers attempted to find ways to assure sustainable forms of financing UNRWA. On March 13, 2018, however, just two days before Rome conference, the USA administration organised a one day 'consultations and brainstorming' at the White House to discuss the future and the humanitarian crisis of Gaza without the participation of the PA, which is still suspending the political communications with the USA's administration (Baskin, 2018).

The USA's administration attempted to disconnect itself from the ongoing UNRWA's financial crisis, and to raise its 'concerns' about the

66 *Ibrahim Natil*

humanitarian crisis of Gaza while the organisers of Roma conference invited 90 countries, including some Member States of the League of Arab States and the European Union Member States. The PA attended the conference and endorsed UNRWA's requirement for $350 m as Canada, Switzerland, Turkey, Qatar, New Zealand, Norway, South Korea, Mexico, Slovakia, India and France pledged $100 (UN, 2018). This pledged is not enough to keep the same full operations of UNRWA as it was. Fida Amer says, 'the aid cut has already left a negative impact on cooperation between UNRWA and wide spectrums of CSOs as thousands of target groups were deprived from services in the refugee camps in the Gaza Strip' (Amer, 2018).

Alternative engagement

The Palestinians manoeuvred to invest its own radical disagreement with Trump's administration to get the Quartet's members as EU, Russia and UN engaged actively in the 'peace process' or at least to break the USA's sole mediation for peace talks (Hawash, 2018). The Palestinians also led and engaged in a global campaign against Trump's policy on Jerusalem, supported by Palestinian solidarity groups around the world. In December 2017, the PA influenced the Arab League to take the case to the UN Assembly General (UNGA) after the USA's veto in the Security Council against the Palestinian proposal. One hundred and twenty-nine (129) countries of the UNGA voted against Trump's proclamation on Jerusalem. This step negatively affected the image of U.S. foreign policy in the Middle East and Northern Africa. Trump's advisers, however, attempted to underline that the U.S. announcement had no bearing on the final status of the negotiations (Holland, 2017).

The PA also attempted to persuade the Quartet's members to get engaged in a serious dialogue with the US administration to change its decision on Jerusalem (Hawash, 2018). The PA also attempted to intensify its communications with the peace groups of the Israeli society despite the fact of their limited influence over the Israeli decision-making process (Srour, 2018). The PA's leadership, however, has been subjected to political pressure from some European and Arab countries to accept the role of the USA, as Federica Mogherini, the high representative for foreign affairs and security policy said, 'any framework for negotiations must involve 'all partners', 'Nothing without the United States, nothing with the United States alone' (Hawash, 2018).

This was a strong message for the Palestinians that the US could not be excluded and the Quartet would not be reactivated to reform the current mechanism, which has already been outdated, dysfunctional and discredited. The reform should consider cooperated mechanism of the Quartet as (AlGindy, 2012) wrote 'instead of undertaking another vain attempt to 'reactivate' the Quartet, the United States, the European Union, United Nations and Russia should simply allow the existing mechanism to go quietly into the night'. However, the hope to revive the Quartet is impossible now owing to the Russian 'special operations' as the Russian President, Vladimir Putin described. Scholars, (Baunov, 2022) of Carnegie Endowment for International Peace argues:

> Rapidly unfolding events in Russia are effectively transforming the conflict in Ukraine from a "special operation" on someone else's territory into a war to defend supposedly Russian land.

This operation has already completed the circumstances of world order and strengthened Western democracies bilateral cooperation and coordination to face and challenge Russian invasion of a neighbouring sovereign country, who have been supported for many years by the EU and the Western countries to reach a level of reforms to be qualified and compatible in accordance with the western democracies performance of good governance. The EU's Auditors' Court, however, described Ukraine as the most corrupt country in Europe. These challenges of Russia to western democracies forced them to impose economic and political sanctions, which automatically reflected and added to the ineffectiveness and inefficiency of the Middle East Quartet in terms of contributing to solving the Palestine-Israel conflict.

CSOs' public diplomacy vs COVID-19

The Quartet has already failed to assist CSOs and the Palestinian civil society in general; however, CSOs attempted to defy the circumstances by increasing its activities of public diplomacy activities by cooperating with local organisations, the UN, diplomatic missions, donors and international organisations to assist with the challenges and the risks of COVID-19 (Amer, 2021). Palestinian civil society has been playing a significant role in supporting the government's role in dealing with containing the spread of COVID-19. For example, a number of CSOs have been running hospitals, community health centres and clinics. These institutions, however, have been suffering from serious barriers and restrictions owing to political instability, violence, Israeli occupation and dependency on foreign aid (Balousha, 2020).

Palestinian civil society has been living in severe circumstances, including a lack of human security, owing to political shifts and the economic scenario. Violence against women has also been a serious issue owing to the long history of conflict in Palestine/Israel and the current hard socioeconomic situation since the Israeli occupation of the Gaza Strip and the West Bank in 1967. COVID-19 and the Israeli threat to

68 *Ibrahim Natil*

annex 30% of the West Bank territories impose new challenges and serious barriers to CSOs' and women's effective engagement and community participation in the OPT. Natil analyses how these shifts have already imposed a serious challenge for CSOs that provide services to the residents of the sector in various fields, such as education and health, and improving livelihoods, unemployment and infrastructure projects has already challenged their scope of work and intervention.

These circumstances have made Palestinian civil society suffer from a high level of violence, poverty, lack of opportunities and absence of hope. These impacts are further implied in contexts of fragility, conflict, refuge, displacement and emergencies, where social cohesion is already undermined and institutional capacity and services are limited. Despite these significant deliveries and contributions by the Palestinian CSOs during the pandemic, they have been facing major challenges as a result of the repercussions of the successive crises striking the Palestinian community owing to the currently harsh economic, social, political and funding shifts resulting from the siege that has been ongoing since 2005. The Society Voice Foundation (SVF), a Gaza-based CSO, addresses many important topics to raise awareness about women and society fighting violence against women during the pandemic and to promote women's social and political participation at all levels. CSOs' staff and volunteers work from home and engage with their society through the internet, and some CSOs run awareness through social media.

Natil (2021) discusses CSOs' engagement with local and international media during COVID-19. Natil also discusses in his book, 'Conflict, Civil Society, and Women's Empowerment: Insights from the West Bank and the Gaza Strip', that CSOs, using social media like Zoom and Facebook, continue to run some online sessions to raise awareness about fighting violence against women during the pandemic. CSOs continued working with marginalised and vulnerable groups of women in the wider society who were hoping for and seeking a better life and ran local activities to defy and challenge the shifts. SVF, for example, also succeeded in implementing eight public online meetings to discuss the mechanisms of participation in decision-making, the role of the media, the empowerment of women and the promotion of human rights and community peacebuilding during the pandemic. These included implementing psychological and social support sessions for children who are in need of play, having fun and carrying out some activities during the pandemic.

Conclusion

The Palestinian society is considered a nationalist and polarised one, owing to the conflict in the region. Foreign aid, however, remains very essential for Palestinian CSOs deliveries, programmes and contributions to their citizens. Many CSOs could not implement their operations or function properly without international aid assistance. In addition to this, UNRWA's budget, which supports the delivery of core essential services for a major segment of Palestinian civil society operates with a large shortfall as the USA cut aid to UNRWA.

CSOs continued their engagement with international civil society organisations and the broader global audiences via social media and technology as part of their public diplomacy activities despite the reduction of foreign aid and the failure of the Middle Quartet to end the conflict and to assist in empowering civil society in Palestine. There have been many scholars who criticised the dysfunctional and outdated mechanism and role of the Middle East Quartet. It has already failed to achieve its own mandate of contributing to solving the Palestinian-Israel conflict as Tocci (2013) writes, the 'Quartet has neither become a genuinely multilateral forum, nor has it been effective in pursuing the goal of a two-state solution in the Middle East'. Different interests of the Quartet's members undermined its coordinated mechanism as a multilateral form to achieve its own mandate to end the violence in Palestine and to assist the Palestinians to improve their own economy. The Quartet has already failed to put pressure on Israel to end occupation according to international law and all UN resolutions in terms of Palestine.

The Quartet's boycott of Hamas' government was a mistake as Tony Blair admitted. This mistake imposed a major challenge to Hamas' transition from violence into a political governing authority as the embargo of the Quartet on it and its government at all levels. Hamas rejected Quartet's demands to compromise its ideology in order to become a legitimate political player, according to the values and norms of world politics. Hamas had made its decision to administer the PA's institutions, despite the fact that for some time it had fought the existence of the PA as the result of the 'taboo agreement' of Oslo, which had compromised the historical parts of Palestine where Israel was established in 1948. The PA, however, was built on the values, cultures and literature of the Oslo peace process, and the Oslo agreement was the essential and basic reference for the PA in all its manifestation, functions and directions, based on the renunciation of violence, the acceptance of Israel's existence, and agreeing to coordinate with Israeli forces at both the civil and military levels.

Its decision to govern Palestinian public institutions was a real challenge for the demands of the international community. Hamas intended to promote its image as a legal organisation, not as a 'terrorist organisation' – as it was considered by the USA, UK and EU. It intended to represent the Palestinian people through its administration of the PA. Hamas thought it could manage international communications and

70 *Ibrahim Natil*

relationships with the international community easily, without compromising its ideology and political standpoints. However, Hamas' image was that of a force dedicated to wiping Israel off the world map. Most ordinary Palestinian people were not fully aware of the complexity of global politics. They were eager for a change and did not realise what would happen next. Hamas rejected calls by the Quartet to moderate its political ideologies.

As a consequence, Hamas began to face harsh criticism from a Palestinian public who were suffering deteriorating economic conditions because of the political deadlock with the Quartet. Palestinians in the Gaza Strip suffered extreme hardship and humanitarian challenges as a result of the embargo. More importantly, Hamas' supporters and constituencies accepted its role as a full political player, despite its political rhetoric of resistance and the use of violence to liberate all Palestine. The PA, however, failed to persuade other actors from the Quartet to take the USA's role or get engaged in the 'process' after Trump's decision on Jerusalem; however, the proclamation assisted the Palestinian popular 'non-violent protests' against the Israeli occupation and promotion of their connection to their causes of Jerusalem and refugees.

The political decisions, and behaviour of Trump, in this regard also reflected all leaks of the so called 'ultimate deal' by removing the question of Jerusalem and refugees from the table of the 'peace process'. This led to complicate the process itself of resolving the Palestinian-Israeli conflict in the near future and pushed the Palestinian leadership to remove itself from U.S. engagement in the process in the short term. This has left, however, a negative impact on already limited alternatives of PA and its capacity to manoeuvre in the absence of Palestinian unity and end the internal division between Gaza and the West Bank. The Palestinians should increase their support for UNRWA's work through their own networks globally as well.

The Palestinian leadership and the civil society, however, need to find an alternative to avoid the negative impacts of Quartet conditions and the US populism on the Palestinian interests as many Palestinian activists still believe. They should try to avoid the same dynamics of populism and to prevent US policy from undermining Palestinian rights and interests as Mohammed Masharqa says, Palestinians should think out of the box to consider alternatives of restructuring the Palestinian-Israeli conflict within a framework of a modern federal state of Palestine and Israel, similar to the Swiss module to promote coexistence and development in the region. Many Palestinians now look to a one-state solution rather than the 'two states' promoted by the international community. Israel has basically rejected a two-state approach since 1999. The people of occupied Palestine will never give up on their legitimate rights, including the right to return to their land. The international

Barriers to CSOs' public diplomacy 71

community needs to understand this, and then put pressure on Israel to end its deliberate targeting of civilians and respect the Palestinians' right to self-determination and statehood. If the West really wants to de-escalate the current situation and save lives, a good place to begin would be for European countries and the US to recognise the State of Palestine without delay.

This political context of the USA's radical change on Jerusalem has been challenged by the Palestinian's 'rejectionist policy' while the USA cut its aid to the institutions of the Palestinian Authority, some CSOs and mainly the *(UNRWA)*. These positions and behaviours have already affected the deliveries of these institutions in the relevant fields of peacebuilding, development and human rights in Palestine. These positions of 'radical disagreement' and 'rejection', however, should generate creative dialogue between two parts to understand deep cultural and political difference, where social media can contribute to promote the values and other many progressive norms of engagement. However, western democracies' sanctions on Russia, in response to its war in Ukraine have already affected the future of the Quartet's and its legitimacy of existence. The war on Ukraine and the increasing competitions of great powers in the Middle East.

References

Abbot, W., and Snidal, D. (1998) Why States Act Through Formal Organizations. *Journal of Conflict Resolution*, 42(1): 3–32.

Al Samak, H. (March 27, 2018). Interviewed. Civil Society Activist, Palestine

AlGindy, K. (2012) The Middle East Quartet: A Post-Mortem. The Brookings Institution https://www.brookings.edu/wp-content/uploads/2016/06/02_middle_east_elgindy_b-1.pdf (Accessed on June 10, 2018)

Amer, F. (February 7, 2018) Interviewed. Director, Society Voice Foundation, Palestine

Baliamoune-Lutz, M. (2016) The Effectiveness of Foreign Aid to Women's Equality Organisations in the MENA. *Journal of International Development, J. Int. Dev.*, 28: 320–341, Published online 29 March 2016 in Wiley Online Library (wileyonlinelibrary.com)

Balousha, H. (2020) Palestinian media discourse during the Covid-19 crisis: A lost opportunity to restore public confidence, paper presented at the Palestinian NGOs Network meeting, 2020.

Baskin, G. (2018) In Maryland, Taking on AIPAC, Jerusalem Post, Available [online] from http://www.jpost.com/american-politics/8-reasons-why-trumps-john-bolton-appointment-is-causing-a-frenzy-among-jews-546961?obOrigUrl= true [Accessed 15 March 2018].

Baunov, A. (2022) Why Is Putin Upping the Ante in Ukraine? The Carnegie Endowment for International Peace. https://carnegieendowment.org/politika/experts/1030 (Accessed on September 30, 2022).

72 Ibrahim Natil

Ben-Ami, S. (2006) *Scars of War. Wounds of Peace: The Israeli–Arab Tragedy*, Oxford: Oxford University Press. p. 324.

Bouchard, C., and Peterson, J (2010) Conceptualising Multilateralism- Can we all just get along?, *MERCURY e-paper*, No. 1, February 2010

Government of Sweden. (2018) Sweden, Jordan and Egypt to hold an extraordinary ministerial meeting to mobilise support for Palestine refugees. Available [online] from http://www.government.se/press-releases/2018/03/sweden-jordan-and-egypt-to-hold-an-extraordinary-ministerial-meeting-to-mobilise-support-for-palestine-refugees/ [Accessed 15 March 2018].

Hawash, K. (2018) The Middle East Quartet still includes the US, so can it still play a role in the peace process? Al Monitor > https://www.middleeastmonitor. com/20180209-the-middle-east-quartet-still-includes-the-us-so-can-it-still-play-a-role-in-the-peace-process/ (Accessed on June 18, 2018)

Holland. (2017) In break with decades of U.S. policy, Trump to recognize Jerusalem as Israel's capital, Reuters. Available [online] from https://www.reuters.com/article/us-usa-trump-israel/in-break-with-decades-of-u-s-policy-trump-to-recognize-jerusalem-as-israels-capital-idUSKBN1DZ04V [Accessed 31 March 2018].

Independent. (2018) Trump administration cuts aid to Palestinians by more than half. Available from: https://www.independent.co.uk/news/world/americas/us-politics/trump-palestine-aid-payments-money-cut-half-un-fund-latest-a8162876.html [Accessed 23 March 2018].

International Crisis Group. (January 26, 2004) *Dealing with Hamas*. Middle East Report N 21.

Lipson, Charles (1991) Why Are Some International Agreements Informal? *International Organization* 45(4): 495–538.

Morningstar, R. (2004) World order unilateralism v multilateralism, Harvard International Review, October 6, 2004 > http://hir.harvard.edu/article/?a=1268 [Accessed 1 June 2018).

Natil, I. (2014) A Shifting Political Landscape: NGOs' Civic Activism and Response in the Gaza Strip, 1967–2014. *Journal of Peace Building & Development*, 9(3): 82–87.

Natil, I. (2015) *Hamas Transformation: Opportunities and Challenges*, Cambridge Scholars Publishing

Natil, I. (2016) The Challenges and Opportunities of Donor-Driven Aid to Youth Refugees in Palestine. *Journal of Peace Building and Development*, 11(2): 78–82

Natil, I. (2022) Israeli military attacks are an affront to human rights. Independent Australia. https://independentaustralia.net/life/life-display/israeli-military-attacks-are-an-affront-to-human-rights,16763 [accessed on September 30, 2022].

Quartet Office (2018) Jerusalem, 2018 http://www.quartetrep.org/page.php?id= 5eb312y6206226Y5eb312 [Accessed 18 June 2018)

Ruggie, G. (1992) Multilateralism: The Anatomy of an Institution. *International Organization*, 46(3): 561–598.

Siegman, H. (2006) Hamas: The Last Chance for Peace? New York Times Review. 53, http://www.nybooks.com/articles/2006/04/27/hamas-the-last-chance-for-peace/ [Accessed 19 June 2018).

Srour, M, (February, 27, 2018) Interviewed. A field researcher at a local human rights organisation, Palestine

Tocci, N. (2011) The EU, the Middle East Quartet and (In) effective, Multilateralism, MERCURY E-paper No.9 June 2011, < accessed June 1, 2018 http://www.iai.it/sites/default/files/mercury-epaper_09.pdf

Tocci, N. (2013) *The Middle East Journal*, 67(1): 28–43 (16), Middle East Institute, 10.3751/67.1.12

UN. (2018) Welcoming $100 Million Pledged for Palestine Refugee Agency. Available from https://www.un.org/press/en/2018/sgsm18952.doc.htm [Accessed 30 March 2018].

7 Civil society organisations' public diplomacy and youth political participation in Egypt

Ahmed El Assal and Amr Marzouk

Introduction

The authors examine how political shifts impact donors driven civil society efforts in the realm of youth political participation programmes. And how do regimes reshape youth participation initiatives to support their rhetoric and gain regime loyalty? The authors argue that the increasing emphasis on the participation agenda and the role of CSOs in promoting youth participation and youth diplomacy, should not be seen in isolation from the rapid transformation of civic spaces, especially in the global south, where formal and informal institutions are used to co-opt CSOs and youth segments to ensure loyalty to the ruling regimes.

This chapter is based on a single case study research, and Egypt serves as the leading case of analysis. While the main time frame of this paper is between 2014–2020, the authors trace back some of the state tactics implemented during the Mubarak regime to shed light on similar patterns towards youth co-optation. The authors use a multi-method approach combining process tracing of the state, donors and CSOs' engagement in the aftermath of the 2011 uprising, in addition to a legal analysis of two recent legislation that impacted youth and civil society participation, law no. 149 of 2019 of CSOs and youth institutions law no. 218 of 2017. The authors draw their analysis and evidence from secondary data, including the OECD funding dataset, national news platforms, CSOs statements and a literature review of previous scholarly work on youth political participation in the wake of the 2011 uprising in Egypt.

The chapter is structured as follows: first, the authors give an overview of the literature on public diplomacy, civil society and youth participation. Second, they discuss donors' role in funding civil society organisations initiatives to support youth political participation after 2011 uprising. Then, the chapter presents a summary of scholarly work on youth participation during the 2011 uprising in Egypt. Following, it discusses shrinking civic spaces in Egypt through newly enacted legislation that limit the role of CSOs in political activities, as well as the new

DOI: 10.4324/9781003441465-7

Civil society organisations' public diplomacy   75

youth centres law that also controls political discussions in formal youth spaces. The final section discusses initiatives initiated by the state to promote youth participation and how this aimed to create a new youth elite aligned with the state's nationalistic and security discourse and ensures loyalty to the regime.

Public diplomacy, civil society organisations and youth participation

The concept of public diplomacy has witnessed many changes and modifications since its first inception by Edmund Gullion in 1965. Gullion, an academic and former diplomat, perceived public diplomacy as a mode of direct interaction between international actors and the foreign public to achieve these actors' goals (Samei, 2015, P.113). This definition was produced during the cold war, and it shows its blunt association between the international goals of the actors and the public, bypassing the governments of these publics completely. Tuch (1990:3) provided another definition of public diplomacy, describing it as a process where a state communicates its ideals, goals, cultures and institution to a foreign public. Some definitions focus on the image and the branding; for example, McQuail (2010) defines public diplomacy as "efforts by nations to win support and a favourable image among the general public of other countries" (P.586 cited in Lengel et al., 2012, p2). Furthermore, as argued by Pultz (2012), public diplomacy differs from traditional diplomacy in that it focuses on all that is public, such as civil societies, religion and culture. Cull (2008) provided five elements of public diplomacy listening, advocacy, cultural diplomacy, exchange diplomacy and international broadcasting.

However, the definition of public diplomacy now is compatible with the changes in our reality. The definition this chapter will use is that of Bruce Gregory who identified public diplomacy as an instrument used by states, associations of states, and some sub-state and non-state actors to understand cultures, attitudes and behaviour; to build and manage relationships; and to influence thoughts and mobilise actions to advance their interests and values. What is interesting about this definition is that it focuses on the tool's aspect of diplomacy instead of focusing on the goal of such diplomacy. This change of focus allows for exploring non-state actors such as CSOs. Another interesting aspect of such a definition is that it moves the focus to "values" instead of "goals". This reflects the emergence of international civil society with its own set of norms and values for instance "human rights" or "cross-cultural dialogue."

Due to the newcomers to the global public arena, CSOs as non-state actors and due to the new changes in the mode of communication (the internet), public diplomacy is no longer a one-way street with the aim of

76 Ahmed El Assal and Amr Marzouk

convincing; instead, it aims to improve communication (Castells, 2008). For Castells, the new public spaces allow and aim to increase communication within the global space and to create a common language between actors in such a space (Castells, 2008). All of these changes allowed for new fields of public diplomacy to emerge, from sport public diplomacy (Horton, 2008; Garamvölgyi et al., 2022), cyber public diplomacy (Cull, 2013), Youth Diplomacy (Tran et al., 2022).

Supporting participation and inclusion of marginalised and vulnerable groups in decision-making, and ensuring that their voices are heard, became an essential element of CSOs work to spread democratic norms as part of the participatory democracy turn (Bherer et al., 2016). In non-democratic regimes, political participation often takes place beyond the formal participation institutions such as electoral process or party politics and includes other forms of informal participation, unruly politics and protests, or participating through CSOs (Schlozman et al., 1997). Political participation often refers to citizen actions that aim to influence political outcomes (Goroshit, 2016). In this chapter, the authors will focus on youth diplomacy, and donors' support of CSOs projects as a field of public diplomacy. The authors argue that the closing down of civic spaces and the state control of youth projects affects the chances of public diplomacy between the European Union (EU) donor countries and Egypt.

CSOs became an engine for youth civic engagement and participation in the social and political realm (United Nations, 2015). However, civic spaces have been shrinking and civil society organisations are facing significant challenges, whereas spaces and agency of CSOs are becoming strictly controlled. According to CIVICUS state of civil society report, the past decade has witnessed a sustained trend of civic space crackdown with new tactics of restrictions, including increasing use of online attacks, censorship, surveillance, restricting protests and fake news laws (CIVICUS, 2021; Hellmeier et al., 2021). Other organisations like Freedom House and V-Dem Democracy Report documented the increasingly democratic and freedom decline as well as the assault on civic spaces in their reports "democracy and pluralism are under assault" (Repucci, 2020) and "Autocratization Turns Viral" (Alizada et al., 2021). A wide range of civil society actors is prone to these restrictions, including youth and activists' groups working on gender equality and women's rights, labour rights, fiscal and economic governance, energy subsidies and land reform, in addition to journalists, scholars and other advocates for social and economic justice (Hossain & Khurana, 2019; Bossuyt & Ronceray, 2020).

Despite the relative expansion of the civil society sector in the MENA region after the Arab Spring protests, these changes have escalated tensions in the relationship between the state and CSOs, particularly for

Civil society organisations' public diplomacy 77

civil society initiatives that depend on foreign funding (Tauber et al., 2019). Several political barriers hinder the impact CSOs may achieve in promoting democracy and fostering participation. The shifts in the political landscape in many developing countries limit the activities of such organisations (Natil et al., 2020). This chapter considers these increasing challenges to CSOs and how it impacts the initiatives aimed at promoting youth participation, particularly in the political sphere. The authors look at the concept of public diplomacy and its linkages to CSOs as influential non-state actors amid these political dynamics.

Overall, there has been growing attention in academic and policy-making circles on youth and the impact of their participation in society's stability. This attention is mainly driven by the global youth surge and the challenges that hinder their active engagement and participation. An increasing correlation is drawn between the youth bulge, youth unemployment and state stability (Oosterom, 2018). Often young people are positioned culturally as naive and immature, excluded from political institutions and cut off from economic resources. They are largely ex-cluded from the formal decisions that affect their future and all of society (Hussain et al., 2020). As Natil explains "youth's" engagement with and contribution to development play a crucial role in international devel-opment; however, they have a limited impact on policy and practice and, ultimately, the lives of poor youths owing to a lack of effective en-gagement, policies, and opportunities' (Natil, 2021, p. 2). Moreover, evidence has shown that lack of political participation and increasing economic and political grievances are breeding grounds for young people to join radical groups (United Nations, 2015). Hence, in transition phases, spreading democratic norms through supporting youth political and civic engagement is a long-term development intervention to safe-guard peace and stability.

Donors support for youth programmes post 2011-uprising

Following the 2011 uprising, several international, regional and local CSOs designed and supported youth programmes to foster youth partic-ipation in the civic and political spheres. The influential role youth played in the mobilisation of the 18 days of protests, as well as the political events that occurred after removing Mubarak from power, was remarkable. Donors and international organisations play a significant role in sup-porting youth development programmes. Nonetheless, the impact of donor-driven youth participation and civic engagement programmes remains contested (Orrnert, 2018). After the 2011 revolution, many western governments saw improving the youth situation in the region as necessary for global and regional stability. Most western countries, including the donor community, have portrayed the Arab Spring mainly

78 *Ahmed El Assal and Amr Marzouk*

as a political struggle between the protesters seeking democratic change and authoritarian regimes failing to address social contract with emerging young generations (Mulderig, 2013). This narrative has also shaped the response of the donor community toward supporting the democratisation process in Egypt.

This raise and soon fall of civil society projects, and youth development is also reflected in the amount of funding received for such projects from the EU. The funding towards democratic participation and civil society saw its highest point during the 2011 revolution. From then, it kept declining, reaching its lowest point in 2011. Same with funding towards the human rights sector, we can see it has declined after reaching its highest levels in 2011.

Directly after the uprising, the majority of traditional aid donors' funds channelled to CSOs were heavily politicised; a significant amount of donor funds was allocated to human rights and civic education programmes that mainly targeted youth and women. The Egyptian government did not welcome the influx of foreign aid to CSOs, for both local and international organisations. As a result, several formal and informal practices were imposed by the state to limit the funds channelled for CSOs including smear campaigns, and the arrest of aid workers in the foreign fund case (173), among other intimidation practices (Elassal & Marzouk, 2020). However, many CSOs, that primarily worked on democracy promotion adopted several strategies to counter the restrictions (Elassal, 2019).

In the period between 2011–2014, several donors heavily supported initiatives that prioritise civic engagement and political participation of youth groups. Youth civic engagement and education constituted the main priority for most of the donor agenda. In March 2011, the United States Agency for Development (USAID) announced the allocation of 65 million USD to democratic and governance programmes in Egypt. According to the USAID foreign assistance data, between 2011 and 2014, at least six projects were funded to strengthen youth political and civic participation with approximately 10 million USD funds. Moreover, according to the open data platform, the Swedish International Development Cooperation Agency (SIDA) has supported CSOs that promote democracy and human rights with approximately 18 million USD between 2011 and 2014. However, these numbers have dropped significantly from 2015 to date.

Additionally, the Middle East Partnership Initiative (MEPI) launched a grant program with a priority area that focuses on the expansion of opportunities for youth, particularly those that provide practical, hands-on experience in civic engagement, public service and volunteerism and that help to improve local communities. Similarly, the European Union (EU) launched another grant scheme for non-state actors and local

Civil society organisations' public diplomacy 79

authorities aiming to encourage inclusive and participatory dialogue with authorities at the local level to discuss and solve shared economic and social problems, especially in marginalised and/or rural areas; promote democratic education and participation of children and youth. Many other donor initiatives were also launched to foster and facilitate youth engagement in the public realm. A flagship program such as the Danish Arab Partnership Program (DAPP) is another funding mechanism that mainstreams youth among all its interventions, among which the human rights and governance pillar received about 38% of its funding, which is the highest amount among its four programme pillars (DAAP, 2015). It should be noted here that these are just examples of the efforts initiated by the donor community to support youth initiatives in civic and political participation and not a systematic review of donor funding to youth CSOs. The lack of available data on youth programmes' funding makes it challenging to conduct such a systematic task.

In the following sections, the authors argue that despite this increasing donor interest in supporting and funding youth political and civic participation through CSOs, the impact and sustainability of this support were limited. Donors support for CSOs in Egypt has already been declining since the crackdown on civil society activities in 2014. Many foreign donors who had invested in Egypt after the revolution froze their politically-related activities or chose to withdraw from Egypt entirely (Brechenmacher, 2017). This limited impact and role for CSOs in advancing the youth participation agenda in Egypt should be seen in light of the state's efforts to close the civic and political spheres. In the next section, we delve into two main strategies adopted by the state to take over the lead in promoting youth political participation. First, introducing restrictive legislation that prohibits any activities of political nature in CSOs or youth centres. Second, the state and its security apparatus carefully selected the initiation of youth political programmes to be at the forefront of youth participation in both the civic and political realms.

New era of youth participation in the wake of the 2011 uprising

The Arab Spring came as a surprise for everyone, started with the Tunisian revolution and was followed by Egypt, Libya, Yemen and Syria. What was labelled then as the "Arab Spring" challenged the arguments about "Arab exceptionalism", this idea that Arab countries will never get rid of authoritarian regimes (Harik, 2006). Youth constituted a large segment of protestors that sparked the 2011 revolution in Egypt and the Arab world (Abdalla, 2016). The 25th of January uprising has been portrayed as a youth revolution where many youth groups were at the forefront of the revolution mobilisation and organising. The majority of youth who have

80   Ahmed El Assal and Amr Marzouk

participated in the revolution define themselves as the revolutionary youth "a readily recognised set of activists who became a highly visible fixture on the country's national political scene and an outspoken voice of opposition" (Rennick, 2018:1). Lack of political participation, high rates of unemployment and underemployment and invasive political and economic corruption motivated young people to engage actively in the revolution, ask for social and political change, and express their grievances. Youth who participated in the demonstrations of Egypt's 2011 revolution felt that the government had not provided them with the economic opportunities they deserved. They have also left excluded and ignored from the formal political sphere and other forms of political participation.

For example, young people were excluded from any meaningful political and civic participation during the Mubarak regime. The National Democratic Party (NDB) leadership and former ousted president Mubarak always used youth participation and empowerment as a dominant narrative – when talking publicly about youth affairs – yet the reality was far from the rhetoric. Presidential speeches calling for broader youth participation, the NDP programme for youth empowerment, and the establishment of the Ministry of Youth were all used as the regime's rhetoric toward empowering youth. Wardany, however, argues that the disconnect between the Mubarak regime's rhetoric and the reality of youth participation was due to four main factors: "the failure of the political leadership to develop a national policy on youth; the instability of the organisational structures supporting youth affairs; and the inadequacies of the legislative framework governing the youth movement in Egypt" (2012:p. 37). The perception of youth problems by the NDP left much to be desired, although the NDP leaders constantly boasted of the increased ratio of youth in the 18–40 age group in the party, which stood at 49.4 per cent of the total membership in October 2008, the party's interest in youth was mainly for propaganda purposes (Ibid, 2012, p. 38)

Numerous youth groups, mainly in youth movements, played a crucial role in preparing and mobilising for the 2011 events, either through traditional means or using new social networking technologies. However, most of these groups were not affiliated with traditional civil society groups such as CSOs or participated in the welling of their political parties' leaders (Ezbawy, 2012). Previous literature dealing with youth participation has looked at young people as either apolitical and disengaged from political life on the one hand or actively participating and engaged in new forms of politics on the other hand (Farthing, 2010). During the Egyptian revolution, both politically engaged youth, as well as apolitical youth joined forces together, seeking the same goal. While a small group of politically active youth were at the core of the 2011 mobilisation, the snowball effect of using social media, i.e., Facebook and Twitter, expanded to a broader circle of apolitical youth who were motivated by their

Civil society organisations' public diplomacy 81

pressuring problems (Ezbawy, 2012; Khamis & Vaughn, 2013). The revolution, however, has expanded the participation of young people in the public sphere, who usually were not active before the 25th of January. Many social and political youth groups emerged from the Tahrir Square events. Nevertheless, ten years later, the majority, if not all, of these groups almost vanished (Rennick, 2018). Spaces and forms of youth participation have changed drastically over the last decade. Although youth have played an active role in the revolution, it has not significantly impacted their political participation and representation. The few years after the revolution witnessed an unprecedented interest and high turnout from young people towards political participation. Nevertheless, participation in formal or informal political events has declined significantly. For example, since 2014, youth participation in electoral events did not reach more than 27% for presidential elections and 20% for parliamentary elections of all voters (Osman & Girgs, 2016).

Youth political participation in the aftermath of the 2011 uprising received increasing scholarly attention. Abdalla (2016) examines the different strategies adopted by youth movements in the transition phase following the protests. He argues that while some strategies were successful in some political contexts, they yielded different outcomes when the political context changed. Thus, some strategies were helpful in the short term but were not sufficient in the long term. Sika (2018) investigates the unconventional modes of youth participation in several Arab countries, including Egypt, after the Arab Spring, she concludes that the vibrant Arab street opened spaces for unconventional youth participation. However, these unconventional methods of participation have led to fragmentation and weakness in the civil society sector. Also, the modes of participation highly depended on the varying political context in each of the five countries she investigated. In exploring the forms of youth participation after the revolution, find that while Egyptian youth are still active in online spaces, they engage more cautiously.

Additionally, they argue that youth are still engaged with formal avenues for political participation and civic engagement, yet their participation in electoral processes is limited. Some argue that the socio-economic frustrations of youth, among other masses who participated in demonstrations, were equally important as the failure to engage youth in the political realm. Bradelyy (2012, p.201) argues that "the vast majority of protestors knew nothing of political ideology. They were brought into the streets, not by a burning desire for free and fair elections, but by the dire economic circumstances in which they lived."

For many decades there has been a lack of inclusive political institutions with the ability to incubate the growing numbers of young people in Egypt. The new regime has initiated several initiatives that are

82 Ahmed El Assal and Amr Marzouk

promoted and marketed as new instruments to integrate youth into the political arena. However, as argued later in this paper, most of these initiatives are created to establish a loyal youth elite that is aligned with the regime's agenda. These initiatives have also impacted previous optimism of donors' support to CSOs to promote youth participation and representation. It also impacted the funding for youth programmes to align with the available political spaces and narratives. Moreover, these new initiatives are likely similar to previous efforts of the NDP to co-opt youth into new existing structures organised by the security apparatus.

Restrictive legislation and shrinking spaces for youth participation

Supportive legislation and policies can play a crucial role in empowering young people. While the political empowerment of young people is critical for their meaningful engagement in governance processes, their participation will be curtailed if parallel attention is not given to young people's economic, social and legal empowerment (Walker et al., 2014). During the Mubarak era, successive governments failed to adopt a supportive policy framework for youth participation. The Mubarak regime failed to adopt policies or programmes that engage youth in decision-making processes or structural policy-making mechanisms. Most activities or efforts toward youth engagement were to polish the regime's reputation rather than a meaningful engagement of young people in policy and decision-making. Political parties have also failed to engage youth in their activities or push for legislative changes representing youth voices in decision-making processes. Wardany argues that:

> Under Mubarak, laws concerning the youth were neglected by legislators. No law related to youth was passed during the Mubarak era. Law 77 for 1975, concerning organisations active in the field of youth and sports, of which some provisions were modified in May 1975, remained the only legislative framework organising action concerning youths in Egypt until 2011. (2012:40)

Following the revolution, youth demands were pushed to be included in the formulation of any new constitutions. The 2014 constitution laid the ground for a broader citizen's freedom of expression and participation in the public realm and witnessed progress in terms of youth supportive legal framework. Explicitly, Article 82 requires the state to guarantee the provision of care to young people and to encourage them to participate in voluntary activties and public life (Osman & Girgs, 2016). Moreover, a strong emphasis in the constitution, Article 180, on

Civil society organisations' public diplomacy 83

youth representation in the local administration, the candidacy age has been reduced to 21 and one-quarter of the total local administration elected councils' seats will be provided to youth under the age of 35. In addition, Article 244 of the constitution highlights the state grantee youth representation in the house of representatives.

The operationalisation of these constitutional grantees to a comprehensive action plan to enhance youth representation and active participation has been a failure. Legislative changes in non-governmental organisations (NGOs) laws entail and pose more challenges and restrictions to the operations of the NGOs sector, which was the fuel for pushing the agenda of youth civic participation and political education at different levels. Moreover, new legislative changes for youth centres also limit any prospects for independent political education and any political activity that might occur in such spaces. New legislative changes after 2014 have maintained the same agenda as the NDP and Mubarak era. A traditional way to deal with youth issues is primarily concerned with social and economic issues rather than a comprehensive participation and engagement agenda, which should also entail political and civic engagement.

NGOs are crucial in supporting youth programmes and their active participation in society. Youth-led progressive groups and organisations are critical to ensuring progressive social change. Under Mubarak, laws concerning youth were neglected by legislators. No law related to youth was passed during the Mubarak era. Law 77 for 1975, concerning organisations active in the field of youth and sports, of which some provisions were modified in May 1975, remained the only legislative framework organising action concerning youths in Egypt until 2011 (Wardany, 2012).

Moreover, previous NGOs legislations, namely Law no. 84 of 2002 had many restrictions on the operations of NGOs and the type of activities they could carry out. As such, most NGOs adopted a political agenda primarily focusing on social and economic issues. According to the World Bank, during the Mubarak era, only 122 youth NGOs existed in Egypt (Al Rouby et al., 2007). Other figures show about 310 youth NGOs in Egypt (Kandeel, 2007). Most of these organisations dealt with apolitical youth-related issues, such as education, economic empowerment, sports, culture, etc.

Since 2011, several attempts have been made to adopt a new law to govern the activities of NGOs in Egypt. Despite the restrictive NGO law, Law 84/2002, many CSOs still managed to either get government approvals or take the risk of implementing youth-related programmes that are mainly focused on socio-political issues. Many organisations have adopted different registration modalities to manoeuvre the restrictions of Law 84/2002. In addition, many donors had more flexible mechanisms to provide funds for different forms of CSOs. Only in 2017, the Egyptian president, el-Sisi, approved a new law that organised the

84 *Ahmed El Assal and Amr Marzouk*

work of civil society organisations, known as Law 70 of 2017. However, the law was widely criticised by national and international NGOs due to its repressive nature. The 2019 NGO Law replaces Law No. 70 of 2017, which replaced the Mubarak-era Law No. 84 of 2002. Efforts have been made by the government and the parliament to review this controversial law, given the points of conflict between the government and the NGOs. In 2019, new Law No. 149 of 2019 on the activities of non-governmental organisations was approved by the president. Nevertheless, several conflict issues between the government and the NGOs remain the same, with no significant changes.

The newly approved law still limits NGOs' political or civic education activity. The law conceives a narrow purpose for national and foreign NGOs. Multiple provisions in the law reference "societal development" as the purpose of NGO activities, sidelining organisations that do not fit into the traditional development definition (TIMEP, 2019). Several articles in the law pose significant challenges for NGOs to operate freely and without a clear definition of used terms. Law prohibits domestic and foreign NGOs from pursuing activities that violate "national security," "public order," "public morals," and "national unity." (Law No. 149/2019[15]). Article 15 also forbids NGOs from conducting political activities, entering into agreements with foreign entities, conducting opinion polls and surveys, relying on foreign persons as experts, employees, or volunteers, participating in workshops abroad without prior approval of the Egyptian authorities, and funding election campaigns.

Working on youth civic and political education issues became very sensitive for many NGOs. The restrictive nature of NGO law and the high surveillance of the security apparatus to the activities of NGOs in Egypt limits any significant efforts toward youth participation in the political realm and undermines the role NGOs can play on this front. Since 2015, several NGOs have turned down grants or avoided collaborating with international organisations or donors supporting projects related to engaging youth in any governance or political education-related activities (Elassal, 2019). Due to these restrictions on activities, NGOs can undertake any intervention regarding youth participation programmes, and donors have become more sensitive toward supporting direct youth political participation programmes. It became almost impossible for NGOs to conduct the same activities that they used to implement directly after 2011. With these legislative limitations, most financial support to youth programmes has been diverted towards more apolitical interventions that are, to some extent, aligned with the government agenda.

During the Mubarak regime, youth centres – affiliated with the Ministry of Youth and Sports (MoYS) failed to engage youth in political training or play any supportive role in preparing youth to participate in

Civil society organisations' public diplomacy 85

the political sphere. The NDP and government followed a traditional approach to political and cultural engagement, which focused mainly on 'filling youth time with social and entertainment activities, with the latter dominating activities in the youth camps (Wardany, 2012, p. 40). According to the latest statistics from the Central Agency for Public Mobilisation and statistics, the number of youth centres in Egypt reached 4,331, of which 10.3% were in urban areas, and 89.7% were in rural areas. There has been no significant increase in youth centres since 2004. Youth centres in Egypt are state-run sports and development institutions that are usually visited by hundreds of thousands of young people, mainly men and students, who cannot afford expensive sports clubs.

After the revolution, the nature of the youth centre's role in political education remained the same as Mubarak era. In addition to the restrictions the NGOs law places on the involvement of NGOs – or any other form of civil society organisations, on youth civic and political activities, another new law was ratified by the parliament that also set forward more restrictions on youth political participation. In November 2017, the Egyptian parliament approved Law no. 218 of 2017, known as Youth Institutions Law. The law prohibits exercising any political activity or promoting any political ideologies at youth centres. The law punishes with jail terms of up to one year and/or fines of up to EGP 50,000 (approximately 3,200 USD) those "who engage in activities contrary to the purpose for which the [youth] institution was established." The banning of any political activities in youth centres was usually a political decision during the Mubarak regime to limit any election campaigning activities using the canters. The law limits any political activity in youth centres, including educational or awareness-raising activities meant to promote youth participation in civic and political affairs.

Barriers to youth participation and public engagement

Governments tend to use a top-down approach when designing initiatives that aim for youth participation and representation. The risk with top-down interventions is that they can result in a lack of genuine interaction and youth involvement. However, appropriate measures taken by implementing organisations can mitigate these risks and ensure more meaningful and continued involvement of young people in governance processes (Orrnert, 2018). Participation can be strengthened by including youth in the design, implementation, monitoring, reporting and evaluation of instruments, strategies and programmes. While in consolidated democracies with stable and well-functioning institutions, youth councils offer viable avenues for young people to effectively participate in planning services, review policies and take decisions over budgets allocated for youth.

86 Ahmed El Assal and Amr Marzouk

In contrast, in fragile or transition societies – where political agendas still have power over institutions – national youth councils have functioned primarily as means for co-opting youth activists and controlling their participation in political activities (Oosterom, 2018). In this case, this co-optation exceeded the traditional official youth councils of the ministry of youth and sports. Also, it included other initiatives sponsored directly by the state and the security apparatus to create its elite youth groups. Despite different regime structures, looking at regime's strategies towards youth participation, it is notable that in principle there are similarities in the rhetoric of youth participation while also state practices to co-opt youth are relatively different.

During the previous regime, youth policies and programmes mainly targeted specific youth segments. Changes introduced to youth-related policies aimed to serve the ruling party's political agenda, moving toward a more liberal economy. Although the NDP has taken several measures to promote youth participation within the party, it was not an inclusive policy action. Youth political participation in the NDP was not foreseen as a reform action or a meaningful change toward active youth participation; nevertheless, it was mainly seen as a contribution to strengthening the party and advancing the personal economic status of its young members (Sika, 2012, p.186). For instance, the NDP launched several youth initiatives to provide youth affiliated with the party with training opportunities and courses (i.e., foreign languages, management skills and ICT) at affordable prices and subsidies (Wardany, 2012). With support from NGOs and the private sector, these initiatives also aimed at promoting private employment rather than dependence on the government. However, such initiatives were used to provide youth with a sense of entitlement due to their party affiliation and help promote the party-political agenda. None of the introduced policies or programmes was designed with the participation of young people. Even the role of youth committees within the party was limited to providing recommendations to the party leadership, but not to being part of any decision-making mechanisms within the party.

Notably, the same rhetoric towards youth participation continued after the 2011 uprising. Although more attention has been pointed to youth due to their prominent role during the 2011 uprising, still strategies of co-optation continued. Five years after the revolution, The state has continuously established youth political initiatives that aim to support the nationalistic discourse since 2014. These initiatives are primarily seen as an effort from the security apparatus to control youth foreseen to take part in any political role in the state apparatus or its various political arms. Incremental initiatives have been launched over the past seven years to consolidate this hegemony of state-sponsored youth in the political and leadership arena.

Civil society organisations' public diplomacy 87

In 2015, the presidential office launched the Youth Leadership Program (YLP) to serve as an academy to create a competent youth base capable of taking charge of political, administrative and social leadership positions. Moreover, since 2016, the government has also initiated five National Youth Conferences and three International Youth Forums, all of which were under the auspices of President with his attendance. Launching the IYF is one of the state's attempts to promote Egypt internationally as a supporter of youth leadership and was primarily organised by the YLP graduates. Members of the YLP who were often invited to the youth forums were promoted to take leadership positions in different ministries, and some have been appointed as deputy governors. Nevertheless, these forums are not seen as spaces where youth can openly critique the government or disagree with its political agenda but rather as superficial platforms to discuss apolitical matters (Wahba, 2017).

These state initiatives have also created another youth political body called the Coordination for Youth Parties and Politicians in 2018. The group was formed from youth represented by different political parties who are affiliated with the state. Over time, the group became an organising body for youth with political aspirations and held nationalistic views in favour of the regime and its security agenda (Mamdouh, 2021). While youth initiatives created by the government have contributed to increasing youth representation in the parliament and representation in several government positions, these efforts are mainly seen as a way to increase loyalty to the regime. One thing that all these initiatives have in common is that it is controlled by the state and aim to create a youth elite that abides by the government narratives.

One major institution that played a role in youth policies in Egypt is the National Academy for Youth Training (NTA). NTA was established with the presidential decree 434 in 2017, and it is a public economic institution headed by the president. According to the Ministry of Finance reports, the Academy is the biggest training institution in Egypt, with a budget of around 901 million Egyptian pounds. The academy is responsible for drawing the youth training policies to all the state institutions (Article 2/343). The Academy is also responsible for the training plans for all the training centres all over the country, and it monitors all the training centres (Article 2/343). The Academy is more attractive for youth to patriciate in, especially since many of its graduates get appointed to senior positions within the administrative body of the state.

Analysing these state efforts in promoting youth programmes should not be isolated from Egypt's broader political and civic restrictions. There has been a crackdown on independent youth movements, university students' groups, and cultural groups and a wider crackdown on online spaces for Youth (Bird, 2016). Thus, strategies to promote youth participation are not different from those that were also promoted by the

88 *Ahmed El Assal and Amr Marzouk*

previous regime. While the tactics and the nature of programmes are significantly different, the aim stays the same to create a youth elite that is loyal to the regime and serves its youth empowerment rhetoric.

Conclusion

The participatory democracy turn scholarship has highlighted the importance of engaging different social groups in decision-making. Low rates of youth participation in formal and informal political processes are notable. CSOs are usually seen as a vehicle to support these participatory avenues from a bottom-up approach. However, civic spaces generally, and CSOs particularly, have been witnessing an increasing legislative and reputation crackdown. Thus, the spaces and agency of CSOs are being challenged in authoritarian contexts. Donors and international organisations supporting democratic promotion programmes and youth activism precisely should bear attention to the political challenges that impact the effectiveness and sustainability of these efforts.

In the Egyptian case, youth played a significant role in mobilising the 25th of January revolution. Youth civic initiatives were at their peak between 2011 and 2013; however, most of these initiatives vanished. Despite donor funding to youth programmes in Egypt, CSOs could not further continue these programmes due to the increasing stifling of the civic and political environment. In contrast, the state has also continued to enact legislations that aim to depoliticise youth civic spaces, either informal through CSOs or formal through the MoYS youth centres. Moreover, several initiatives were established by the state to control youth political participation and create a new youth elite that is aligned with the government's narratives. These efforts have skewed CSOs' role after the 2011 uprising through donor-led youth programmes.

Youth training and capacity-building activities in civic and political engagement, human rights, and electoral processes have increased. The weak role of political parties in youth civic and political rights education before 2011 left a gap that needed to be filled. CSOs stepped in after the uprising to fill this gap by undertaking political education programmes to foster youth engagement in the public sphere. A few years after the revolution, however, shrinking civil society spaces in Egypt made it impossible to continue supporting such activities.

Despite donor funding for youth programmes in Egypt, CSOs could not advance them and consolidate their existence as influential actors in supporting youth participation, mainly due to restrictions imposed on CSOs. In contrast, the state has continued to enact legislation that has depoliticised civic spaces, whether informal (CSOs) or formal (Ministry of Youth and Sports youth centres). Moreover, several initiatives have been launched by the government to control youth political participation

Civil society organisations' public diplomacy 89

and create a new youth elite that is aligned with the government's narratives. These efforts have unsettled the role of CSOs, undertaken through donor-funded youth programmes since the 2011 uprising.

The increasing emphasis on the participation agenda and the role of CSOs in promoting youth participation and youth diplomacy programmes should not be seen in isolation from the rapid transformation of civic spaces, especially in hybrid and semi-authoritarian regimes. In such contexts, formal and informal institutions are used to co-opt CSOs and different youth segments to ensure loyalty to the ruling regimes. Following the 2011 uprising in Egypt, donors have shown an increasing interest in promoting democratic and liberal norms through financing civil society activities. Training and capacity building of youth on civic and political engagement, human rights and electoral processes were increasing. The weak role of political parties in youth civic and political rights education before 2011, has left a gap that should have filled. CSOs stepped in after the uprising to fill this gap by undertaking political education programmes to foster youth engagement in the public sphere. A few years after the revolution, however, shrinking civil society spaces in Egypt made it impossible to continue supporting such activities.

Since 2014, several legal measures and state-led youth initiatives were introduced by the state. These measures stifled the marginal role of donor-supported civil society activities after the revolution in favour of programmes that ensured establishing of a new youth elite aligned and loyal to the regime instead of inclusive youth participation and representation in the public sphere. The political transition and momentum that occurred post-2011 uprising has influenced donor policies to further advocate for youth empowerment and participation in both the economic and political spheres. Directly after the 2011 revolution, the amount of aid funds allocated for youth political engagement was heavily focused on democratic inclusion and participation. Yet, these efforts also became limited by the restrictions imposed by the state on the broader civic and political society. In the meantime, notably, donors' support to youth programmes in Egypt shifted from politically driven youth development to more apolitical programmes – more likely to focus on skills and employment and less on political participation, engagement and empowerment.

References

Abdalla, N. (2016). Youth Movements in the Egyptian Transformation: Strategies and Repertoires of Political Participation. *Mediterranean Politics*, 21(1), 44–63.

Al Rouby, H., Samra, M., Helmy, G., & Refay, M. (2007). *Mapping of Organisations Working with and for Youth in Egypt*. World Bank: Capacity Building and Knowledge-Sharing Partnership Program for Youth Organizations.

90 Ahmed El Assal and Amr Marzouk

Alizada, N., Cole, R., Gastaldi, L., Grahn, S., Hellmeier, S., Kolvani, P.,... & Lindberg, S. I. (2021). Autocratization turns viral. *Democracy report*.

Bherer, L., Dufour, P., & Montambeault, F. (2016). The Participatory Democracy Turn: An Introduction. *Journal of Civil Society*, *12*(3), 225–230.

Bird. (2016). Loyal youth, model citizens [Online] Available at: https://www.madamasr.com/en/2016/02/14/feature/politics/loyal-youth-model-citizens/

Bossuyt, J., & Ronceray, M. (2020). *Claiming Back Civic Space*. ECPDM

Brechenmacher, S. (2017). *Civil Society Under Assault: Repression and Responses in Russia, Egypt, and Ethiopia*. Washington, DC: Carnegie Endowment for International Peace.

Castells, M. (2008). The New Public Sphere: Global Civil Society, Communication Networks, and Global Governance. *The Annals of the American Academy of Political and Social Science*, *616*(1), 78–93.

Cull, N. J. (2008). Public Diplomacy: Taxonomies and Histories. *The Annals of the American Academy of Political and Social Science*, *616*(1), 31–54.

Cull, N. J. (2013). The Long Road to Public Diplomacy 2.0: The Internet in US Public Diplomacy. *International Studies Review*, *15*(1), 123–139.

CIVICUS. (2021). *2021 State of Civil Society Report*. Johannesburg: CIVICUS.

DAAP. (2015). *Final Evaluation of the Arab Danish Partnership Program 2012-2015*. Copenhagen: Danida.

El Assal, A. (2019). 'Human rights organizations and navigating the political configuration of power in post-2011 egypt'. In Natil, I., Pieroban, C., & Tauber, L. (eds.), *The Power of Civil Society in the Middle East and North Africa: Peacebuilding, Change, and Development*. London: Routledge.

El Assal, A., & Marzouk, A. (2020). 'Reinvention of nationalism and the moral panic against foreign aid in Egypt'. In Natil, I., Malila, V., & Sai, Y. (eds.), *Barriers to Effective Civil Society Organisations: Political, Social and Financial Shifts*. London: Routledge.

Ezbawy, Y. A. (2012). The Role of the Youth's New Protest Movements in the January 25th Revolution. *IDS Bulletin*, *43*(1), 26–36.

Farthing, R. (2010). The Politics of Youthful Antipolitics: Representing the 'Issue' of Youth Participation in Politics. *Journal of youth studies*, *13*(2), 181–195.

Garamvölgyi, B., Bardocz-Bencsik, M., & Dóczi, T. (2022). Mapping the Role of Grassroots Sport in Public Diplomacy. *Sport in Society*, *25*(5), 889–907.

Goroshit, M. (2016). Political Participation: A Latent Variable Approach. Testing Measurement Equivalence of Political Participation Using ESS Data. *Eurasian Journal of Social Sciences*, *4*(1), 26–38.

Harik, I. (2006). Democracy, Arab Exceptionalism, and Social Science. *Middle East Journal*, *60*(4), 664–684.

Hellmeier, S., Cole, R., Grahn, S., Kolvani, P., Lachapelle, J., Lührmann, A.,... & Lindberg, S. I. (2021). State of the World 2020: Autocratization Turns Viral. *Democratisation*, *28*(6), 1053–1074.

Horton, P. (2008). Sport as Public Diplomacy and Public Disquiet: Australia's Ambivalent Embrace of the Beijing Olympics. *International Journal of the History of Sport*, *25*(7), 851–875.

Hossain, N., & Khurana, N. (2019). Donor responses and tools for responding to shrinking space for civil society: a desk study.

Civil society organisations' public diplomacy 91

Hussain, R. E., Macmillen Voskoboynik, D., & Mejia Julca, E. (2020). Shaking Up to Move Forward: Visions for Stronger Partnerships between Youth Movements and Social Organisations.

Kandeel, A. (2007). Youth Organizations in Egypt, Cairo: United Nations Fund for Population in collaboration with Arab Network for Civil Society Organizations

Khamis, S., & Vaughn, K. (2013). Cyberactivism in the Tunisian and Egyptian Revolutions: Potentials, Limitations, Overlaps and Divergences. *Journal of African Media Studies*, *5*(1), 69–86.

Mamdouh, R. (2021). The new vanguard? A security-certified youth [Online]. Available at: https://www.madamasr.com/en/2021/03/24/feature/politics/the-new-vanguard-a-security-certified-youth/ [Accessed 28 July 2022].

Mulderig, M. C. (2013). *An Uncertain Future: Youth Frustration and the Arab Spring*. Pardee Paper, N.16, Boston University.

Natil, I. (2021). Introducing challenges to youth civic engagement and local peacebuilding. In *Youth Civic Engagement and Local Peacebuilding in the Middle East and North Africa* (pp. 1–12). Routledge.

Natil, I., Malila, V., & Sai, Y. (Eds.). (2020). *Barriers to Effective Civil Society Organisations: Political, Social and Financial Shifts*. Routledge.

Oosterom, M. (2018). *Youth Engagement in the Realm of Local Governance: Opportunities for Peace?*. IDS.

Orrnert, A. (2018). *Youth Initiatives: Supporting Citizen Engagement with Government and Civic Life*. Research report, GSDRC, Birmingham University.

Osman, M., & Girgs, H. (2016). *Towards Effective Youth Participation*. Cairo: Population Council.

Pultz, K. (2012). Dialogue and Power: Understanding Danish Public Diplomacy Efforts in the Middle East. *The Hague Journal of Diplomacy*, *7*(2), 161–180.

Rennick, S. A. (2018). *Politics and Revolution in Egypt: Rise and Fall of the Youth Activists*. Routledge.

Repucci, S. (2020). Democracy and pluralism are under assault. *Freedom House*.

Samei, M. F. A. (2015). The European Union's Public Diplomacy towards the Arab Spring: The Case of Egypt. *The Hague Journal of Diplomacy*, *10*(2), 111–138.

Schlozman, K. L., Brady, H. E., & Verba, S. (1997). The big tilt. *The American Prospect*, *8*(32), 74–80.

Sika, N.(2012). Youth Political Engagement in Egypt: From Abstention to Uprising. *British Journal of Middle Eastern Studies*, *39*(2), 181–199.

Sika, N. (2018). Civil Society and the Rise of Unconventional Modes of Youth Participation in the MENA. *Middle East Law and Governance*, *10*(3), 237–263.

Tauber, L. (2019). Introduction. *In* Natil, I., Pierobon, C., & Tauber, L. (Eds.) *The Power of Civil Society in the Middle East and North Africa: Peace-Building, Change, and Development*. Routledge.

TIMEP. (2019). TIMEP Brief: Law No. 149 of 2019 (NGO Law) [Online]. Available at: https://timep.org/reports-briefings/ngo-law-of-2019/. [Accessed: 5 September 2020].

Tran, L. T., Bui, H., & Nguyen, M. N. (2022). Youth agency in public diplomacy: Australian youth participation in outbound mobility and connection building between Australia and the Indo-Pacific region. *International Studies in Sociology of Education, ahead-of-print*(ahead-of-print), 1–25.

Tuch, H. N. (1990). *Communicating with the World*. Palgrave Macmillan.

United Nations. (2015). *World Youth Report: Youth Civic Engagement*. New York: United Nations.

Wahba, D. (2017). We need to talk, indeed! [Online]. Available at: https://www.madamasr.com/en/2017/11/15/opinion/u/we-need-to-talk-indeed/. [Accessed 3 August 2022].

Walker, D. et al (2014). *Partners for Change: Young People and Governance in a Post-2015 World*. London: Overseas Development Institute.

Wardany, Y. (2012). The Mubarak Regime's Failed Youth Policies and the January Uprising. *IDS Bulletin, 43*(1), 37–46.

8 Challenges to civil society organisations' public diplomacy

Militarism, restrictions and violence in Libya and Lebanon

Ibrahim Natil

Introduction

The chapter enriches the current debate on CSOs' public diplomacy campaigns by extending it to COVID-19, violence and militarism. It provides the reader with empirically based and up-to-date but scientifically grounded analyses of civil society developments in Libya and Lebanon. It will appeal not only to an academic audience but also to international agencies, policymakers and practitioners active in the specified regions. The purpose of investigation in this chapter is to see to what extent COVID-19 has tested civil society organisations (CSOs) in their scope of work, operations and missions in conflict zones as countries of Libya and Lebanon. The mounting pressures that impacted the everyday work of the CSOs and the shifts and challenges they underwent form the crux of the paper. It also examines some CSOs from each country to identify the differences between cultural contexts, political violence environments and social dynamics to understand these shifts and challenges.

The chapter studies these challenges and how some CSOs have coped with these shifts. This paper also will focus on the political, social and funding shifts and barriers to CSOs in the field of civic engagement and social change based on active grassroots 'participatory democracy' during the pandemic. It is essential to discuss Aragonès and SánchezPagés'concept of 'participatory democracy' as a process of collective decision-making where citizens have the power to decide on change. To conclude, the central argument in the investigation of this main question is contrary to wide assumptions that CSOs in unstable circumstances and divided societies have no room or power to influence society and become engaged in the development of their society or support active participation while enduring uncertainty and shifts emerged during the COVID-19.

Theoretical framework

Several studies suggest that social, political and financial shifts always impose real challenges and barriers to civil society organisations' (CSOs)

DOI: 10.4324/9781003441465-8

94 *Ibrahim Natil*

abilities in general from the Global South as Pádraig Carmody et al. (2020) discuss. Despite the negativity of the pandemic, it still provides opportunities for CSOs to increase their legitimacy and engagement, build new alliances and explore new platforms for digital civic engagement, as Saul Mullard and Per Aarvik (2020) discuss. CSOs usually challenge unexpected circumstances by fostering their abilities to build local partnerships at different scales of governance to drive innovation and provide humanitarian relief in the face of war, natural disasters and other crises (Weeden, 2015).

This chapter studies the civil society shifts, challenges and responses to COVID-19 and its impact of public diplomacy activities. It investigates the following important questions: To what extent has COVID-19 challenged CSOs' scope of work, operations and missions in conflict zones such as Libya and Lebanon? What are the pros and cons of the circumstances resulting from COVID-19 and its impact on the shifts and challenges faced by CSOs in conflict zones? Barriers to effective CSOs are defined as those that affect the ability of this sector to cope with and operate within the shifting landscape, conditions, restrictive political systems, social complexities, cultural contexts and economic circumstances in conflict zones (Natil, 2020:9–17). The COVID-19 pandemic, however, has been an unexpected and very serious barrier to effective CSOs' engagement and public diplomacy activities. The World Health Organization (WHO), however, had declared it a pandemic by the beginning of March 2020 (WHO, 2020).

In the mentioned cases, people's active participation and engagement in CSO activity is a form of 'participatory democracy' that responds to the shifting political landscape (Natil, 2019: 24–38). Hilmer (2010) and Aragones and SánchezPagés (2009) define 'participatory democracy' as a process of collective decision-making where active citizens have the power to decide on change. Active citizens' participation and engagement in local organisations, student unions, political groups, movements and CSOs is a form of 'participatory democracy' in responding to the lack of democratic process in, for instance, a conflict zone, where the political system may not function during the pandemic as well (Natil, 2020).

The third sector comprises non-governmental and not-for-profit organisations, volunteer organisations, charities and CSOs undertaking a diverse mix of support and representation activities with a dedication to a particular societal issue or group in conflict zones. Many of these are brought together voluntarily to work towards collective interests and have long histories of challenging political adversaries, such as with CSOs (Pulla et al., 2019). The third sectors in Western countries, however, are part of active democracies that also engage a range of social and political groups in governments' decision-making processes. However, the pandemic has already caused a human development crisis affecting social groups and

Challenges to civil society organisations' public diplomacy 95

marginalised communities worldwide (UNDP, 2019). The third sector, therefore, has the opportunity during this time to exercise democratic rights to push governments towards collective interests and responsibilities. There are many types of CSO involved in delivering aid, including faith-based groups, trade unions, professional associations and internationally affiliated organisations with branches in many different countries. Furthermore, they have been active contributors to the relief, development and empowerment of civil society despite social, cultural, economic and political shifts and challenges.

This chapter focuses on the political, social and funding shifts and barriers to CSOs in the field of civic engagement and social change based on active grassroots 'participatory democracy' in conflict zones as countries in Libya and Lebanon. The Organisation for Economic Co-operation and Development (OECD) has adopted the following definition of CSOs:

> CSOs can be defined to include all non-market and non-state organisations outside of the family in which people organise themselves to pursue shared interests in the public domain. [...] Examples include community-based organisations and village associations, environmental groups, women's rights groups, farmers' associations, faith-based organisations, labour unions, co-operatives, professional associations, chambers of commerce, independent research institutes and the not-for-profit media
>
> (OECD, 2011).

CSOs attempt to show the advantages of different groups working together for mutual benefit and tangible results to engage victims in participating in social and political activities. The participatory process is also associated with the practice of a top-down mechanism conducted to include citizens' engagement and contribution to the public sector, as (Bherer et al., 2016) argue. The central argument in this investigation of this main issue is contrary to wide assumptions that CSOs in unstable circumstances and divided societies have no room or power to influence society and become engaged in the development of their society or support active participation while enduring uncertainty and shifts as COVID-19 pandemic. Here, it is essential to mention Hilmer's (2010) discussion of the definition and concept of participatory democracy, in which active citizens have the power to decide on change for their future.

The core approach of CSOs' intervention and engagement during shifts can be identified from democracy theory (Paffenholz & Spurk, 2010: 65). CSOs have been considered crucial stakeholders in mobilising and empowering society as key drivers of political, economic and societal change processes in conflict zone as Libya and Lebanon. They deliver

96 Ibrahim Natil

actions in the fields of women's empowerment, civic engagement, community development, human rights, community peacebuilding, conflict resolution, health and sports. CSOs also aim to increase the engagement of marginalised and vulnerable groups in public dialogue, activism and community peacebuilding (Natil, 2014). Sigman and Lindberg (2019), however, argue that an egalitarian democracy is one in which individuals from all social groups are equally entitled and capable of exercising their political rights and freedoms. Only a narrow space, however, is given for civil society to operate freely and effectively, as only 4% of the world's population live in countries where fundamental civil society freedoms, association, peaceful assembly and expression are respected. (CIVICUS, 2019)

Hulme and Horner (2020) discuss the social structural levels affected by the pandemic that has not only transformed social groups but also changed the social, economic and political institutions and norms – essentially, positively or negatively, changing the 'rules of the game'. These tensions have already shaped a new generation of inequalities and the severity of the unfolding human development crisis (UNDP, 2019). The pandemic has exposed harmful effects on the marginalised and vulnerable groups in MENA countries. Pulla, Jaysawal and Saha (2020), however, argue that there have been a number of human rights groups calling for the engagement of such marginalised groups in decision-making processes to provide adequate representation and expression of concern over economic and environmental rights worldwide. This calls civil society's involvement in policy-making throughout the current crisis into question.

The third sector, including CSOs, has valuable experience and expertise in the analysis of structural inequalities that could help to build an understanding of the issues citizens face and to critique the presented solutions. This calls the power of people who decide if those solutions serve the collective interest and the need to propose alternatives into question. The influences on civil societies are presented. During the COVID-19 pandemic, CSOs' typical influences and strategies have included using mass gatherings to bring attention to and advocate for structural changes, along with protesting against potential funding cuts from governments as well as private and international sources due to COVID-19 complications.

CSO activists and ordinary citizens attempt to challenge ineffective, inefficient and insufficient public policies while they still have some influence over processes of change (Paffenholz, 2010). These shifts always affect CSOs, which hinders their ability to perform their work by influencing policy processes that exist in some developing countries owing to the political landscape shifts, such as in the MENA region (Natil, 2020). These processes often undermine and block delivery, engagement and contribution to development and change. The legitimacy question has been a crucial issue in whether CSOs are able to mobilise resources

Challenges to civil society organisations' public diplomacy 97

and generate local support from the general public, philanthropists and the private sector (Wiggers, 2016). Rachel Hayman (2017) has raised the question of the legitimacy, effectiveness and credibility of CSOs. Maysa Jalbout (2020), however, argues that CSOs are a vital part of ensuring that developing regions are not left behind as a result of the pandemic:

> The MENA region's capacity to withstand the impact of COVID-19 on its most vulnerable communities, and face up to other challenges, is conditioned by how significant its support to civil society will be. Millions of Arabs – orphans, refugees, elderly, people with disabilities, widows, and the unemployed – are depending on it.
>
> (Jalbout, 2020).

This chapter takes this further as the societies of Libya and Lebanon have been enduring very severe circumstances owing to economic deterioration, the absence of reconciliation, violence and divisions. These circumstances have already created barriers to effective CSOs.

Methodology

The author reviewed the existing literature and interviewed a number of CSO activists who engaged in activities during the periods of the COVID-19 pandemic and quarantine in Libya and Lebanon. The author also analyses some CSOs' activities, work delivered, statements and literature produced by their representatives and activists from each country. Therefore, the author uses the case study approach to examine the challenges and shifts facing CSOs in different cultural contexts, political environments and social dynamics in these countries. Gerring's (2011) case study approach is used to understand these differences within the subfield of comparative politics. This approach assists us to understand these selected countries, which have been enduring very severe circumstances, owing to economic deteriorations, the absence of reconciliation, violence and divisions. These circumstances have already created barriers to CSOs' operations and deliveries. These countries including their CSOs face unstable political environment and harsh economy. In other words, Gerring's (2011) case study approach also assists the readers to understand different social, political and economic challenges facing CSOs in each country during the COVID-19 pandemic.

Civil society in a divided country

Conflict zones are not helpful for coordination and collaboration between different parties, which are essential to fighting COVID-19, as Peters and El Taraboulsi-McCarthy (2020) discuss. In March 2020, international humanitarian actors reported a total of 851 access

98 Ibrahim Natil

constraints on the movement of humanitarian employers and items within and into Libya (OCHA, 2020). Katie Peters and Sherine El Taraboulsi-McCarthy (2020) have discussed how the COVID-19 pandemic has been used for political gains as accessing healthcare is often severely limited and fuels hatred towards African refugees in Libya. Nada Elfeituri (2020) argues that the grassroots response to COVID-19 covers three main aspects – connecting local politics with national leadership and transnational partnerships, raising awareness on public health issues, and leading humanitarian response efforts in Libya.

The pandemic and conflict, however, present a real threat to life despite the global initiative called for by the United Nations Secretary-General, António Guterres, to end the armed conflict to give priority to saving lives, tackling the pandemic and facilitating delivering critical humanitarian supplies. Civil society actors have been challenged by these barriers and conditions, and Asama Khalifa (2020) notes that Libyan CSOs have been shrinking since 2014 owing to conflict and devastated infrastructure. Elfeituri (2020) however, argues that collaboration between formal institutions and CSOs should be one of the core approaches in conflict areas while tackling the pandemic in Libya.

Peters and El Taraboulsi-McCarthy (2020) however, write that conflict zones always have weak services and infrastructure, and healthcare facilities are thus incapacitated when trying to tackle the spread of the pandemic. The southern area of Libya, for example, is the most vulnerable area, and the people there have no access to services. The government is not functioning owing to the ongoing conflict, as Zorg Madi, programme manager at the Tamazight Women's Movement and member of the Civil Society Platform for Peacebuilding and Statebuilding (CSPPS), states:

> Southern Libya is the most vulnerable place in the country. It has no functioning institutions and no government, as neither is capable of penetrating the area because of the ongoing conflict between the many different militant factions and tribes. The population has practically no access to services. Doctors and equipment are sparse. As of now, there are no confirmed cases of COVID-19 in the South of Libya just yet, but once the virus reaches that region too, the consequences are going to be catastrophic
>
> (De Harder, 2020).

CSOs, however, have the abilities to foster local partnership at different scales of governance to drive innovation and provide humanitarian relief in the face of war, natural disasters and other crises (Elfeituri, 2020). Community activism, local initiatives and voluntary contributions have been visible and significant during the pandemic; for example, a local businessman donated 100 beds to hospitals in Misrata

Challenges to civil society organisations' public diplomacy 99

and volunteers from Mohamed Alhmouzi's local CSO launched a campaign to disinfect public spaces. This engagement shows that the CSOs are always on the frontline of crisis response, and their role during the pandemic is more vital than ever to provided such essentials as healthcare, food and shelter for those in need.

Khalifa (2020) argues that the Libyan government ignores the inclusion of CSOs in its public policies and criticises the government's response to COVID for lacking an engagement of persons with disabilities in tackling the pandemic. 'Access' network, a group of civil society actors, however, launched a social media campaign to raise awareness for those people and engage them in tackling the pandemic. The *t*ransparency of accessing information and data, which is essential to track and contain the spread of COVID-19, is limited in conflict zones (De Harder, 2020). Some regimes have been found to control CSOs' civic space by imposing a system of dominating financial channels (CIVICUS, 2019). Youngs and Panchulidze (2020), however, write that weak democracies and autocracies have used restrictive COVID-19 measures to inhibit democratic activities and silence critical voices. Libyan civil society, for example, is navigating and negotiating a complicated relationship with the military authorities led by Khalifa Haftar, while COVID-19 is being used as an opportunity by Haftar to tighten his authoritarian grip on Benghazi (Elfeituri, 2020).

This limits the civic space that is given to CSOs as an independent actor that assists 'people to claim their rights in promoting rights-based approaches, in shaping development policies and partnerships and in overseeing their implementation' according to Busan Global Partnership Forum for Effective Development Cooperation, (2011). Civil society activists, however, increasingly witness poor public freedom and narrow civic space owing to controlled political systems, socio-political deadlock, conflict and harsh economic life. Challenges and shifts always encourage civil society actors to come forward to deliver services such as relief, health development and empowerment of civil society (Natil, 2019).

Peters and Taraboulsi-McCarthy (2020), however, argue that conflict zones are areas of deep inequalities, which means that access to healthcare is not available to all, if it is present. Women's civil society organisations, for example, take the initiative to implement their own voluntary independent initiatives despite the fact that women are trapped between conflict and health as well as the fact that the government is not gender-inclusive, as Khalifa (2020) discusses. Civil society actors both contribute to stabilising a divided nation while also tackling COVID-19 during the civil war in Libya, as Zorg Madi says:

> The COVID-19 response is not very government driven. Yes, both governments do implement measures, but they often function to

100 *Ibrahim Natil*

oppress the people and reiterate their own legitimacy as the ruling party. But whatever is happening in Libya right now regarding the pandemic is very people-driven, in a very organic way, coming from civil society

(De Harder, 2020).

The pandemic has provided a space for CSOs to foster partnerships to deliver services, share knowledge and mobilise local resources, and they are slowly gaining legitimacy and trust from local communities (Elfeituri, 2020). Many Libyans still *'look at these organisations with suspicious eyes, owing to division, lack of transparency and absence of the state'* (Tomi, 2017). Mobilising resources is a challenge for CSOs as donors have channelled their available resources into emergency pandemic responses. This shift by the donors has led to a massive shrinking of implemented CSO deliveries on the ground and civic activism engagement during the COVID-19 pandemic (Youngs & Panchulidze, 2020).

Despite these obstacles, state powers are responding to the virus, and the holders of resources, CSOs and third sectors across the globe are still coming together with collective interests in mind, although they are not always gathering in person as was previously done. However, CSOs in the countries of the Global South, such as Lebanon, have been active during the pandemic.

Civic activism and the shifting landscape in Lebanon

The COVID-19 global pandemic hit Lebanon while it was going through a complex and unprecedented economic, political and social crisis (UNICEF, 2020). Prior to COVID-19, Lebanon witnessed a serious civil protest against a social media tax, economic hardship and pressing financial concerns (CIVICUS, 2020: p11). Maha Yahya (2020) argues that Lebanon was facing an urgent need for a new social contract, owing to the political and economic model that has distinguished it since its independence in 1943. Lebanon, however, is divided by its complicated demography, social structure, political positions and patronage power that are shared between various sects, including Christians, Shia and Sunni Muslims and Druze. On 17 October 2019, various activists from all across the spectrum, including sectarian communities, led a peaceful civil protest to end the corruption and patronage network of long-term politicians who have controlled the public services, social and political life since the Taif Accord, which concluded the Lebanese civil war (1975–1990) (Yahya, 2020).

However, thousands of Palestinian and Syrian refugees who live in Lebanon did not engage in the civil protest against the political leadership. Palestinian refugees, for example, have been wary of getting involved in

Challenges to civil society organisations' public diplomacy 101

the civil protests as they enjoy a very marginal space in civil society and have often been scapegoated in the national crises and conflict, Stephen McCloskey (2020) argues. The Palestinian refugees who were forced to leave their homes after the establishment of Israel in 1948 are not represented in political and social life. They are also excluded from 36 jobs and live in the informal economy, particularly during the COVID-19 lockdown. Syrian refugees, meanwhile, have taken Lebanon to be a safe shelter since the eruption of the Syria crisis in 2012 despite its weak economy and complicated social structure, as Filippo Dionigi (2016) reveals.

This question has been a crucial issue for debate that has increased the community tension regardless of the pandemic. The pandemic, however, has provided an opportunity for different actors to work together, Mullard and Aarvik (2020) argue. In July 2020, more than 30 partners from different institutions and actors, including UN Lebanon, the government and civil society, launched a campaign to raise citizens' awareness and to tackle the increasing number of people infected by COVID-19 (UNICEF, 2020). Mullard and Aarvik (2020) argue that civil society is exploring new civic spaces through increasing engagement on social media networks during the pandemic. The spread of COVID-19 forced activists to halt their civil protest actions and turn to social media engagement in Lebanon. Freedom of expression is a viable option for articulating citizens' discontent, as Youngs and Panchulidze (2020) discuss.

The crisis has also provided a space for Lebanese CSOs to increase their civic digital engagement. Social media is used to recruit volunteers and raise funds, Amira-Géhanne Khalfallah (2020) reveals. However, there has been a decline in fundamental freedoms and freedom of speech with the help of more aggressive intervention from security services in Lebanese society over the past years. Emily Lewis (2020) discusses civil society and the authoritarian state, cooperation and contestation in this context. The authorities arrested or summoned for interrogation more than 60 democracy and civil protest activists for their social media posts since 17 October 2019 according to (Human Rights Watch, 2020). Hundreds of activists, however, innovated a new approach by using their cars to protest against the government's policy in the pandemic, as online engagement cannot be a substitute for street protests (Youngs & Panchulidze, 2020: 11–20.). Fourteen international and local organisations formed a coalition to defend freedom of expression in Lebanon on 13 July 2020 (Human Rights Watch, 2020).

Lebanese civil society, in the face of crises in daily life, goes from one hardship to another, and the political class has never been so unpopular. The rate of inflation is now 72%, and this has already affected the price of food products (Khalfallah, 2020). CSOs have the ability to organise themselves to face the government's inability to deliver services such as medical equipment and food and to raise awareness as citizens lose hope

102 *Ibrahim Natil*

in the political establishment's and the public institutions' ability to tackle COVID-19. Lewis (2020) also discusses the increasing gender-based violence due to quarantine and the frustration of being locked at home after the government ordered people to 'stay home, stay safe' on 15 March 2020. KAFA, a Lebanese civil society organisation, aims at protecting women from violence, running a 24-hour hotline over the phone and via internet platforms like Skype to provide support services. KAFA reported that, in March 2020, 60% of victimised women who contacted KAFA's hotline for the first time did so due to suffering from physical violence or psychological abuse during the lockdown (Khalfallah, 2020).

Conclusion

Despite the fact that serious challenges have been posed to civil society and CSOs all over the world in general and in the Middle East in particular, CSOs have explored mechanisms, tactics and techniques to accommodate the new context and environment of lockdowns and quarantines in conflict zones. Once again, this shows CSOs' ability to respond with a quick sudden shift on the occurrence of unforeseen events and emergencies, in the absence of democracy, and under repressive regimes. Despite their limited resources during the pandemic, CSOs' responses and engagement in local initiatives and community activism in tackling COVID-19 across various communities in Libya, Palestine and Lebanon have been significant contribution. CSOs have been used to social, political and funding shifts and barriers from time to time. This pandemic, however, surprised not only CSOs but also governments, and they were unprepared. CSOs' staff and volunteers, however, learnt various lessons and experimented by engaging with other CSOs and exchanging information and expertise with them. CSOs' response to the pandemic was to quickly get engaged with its grassroots and target groups. Additionally, CSOs have proven that they are capable of delivering a model of services managed by professional teams during the pandemic. However, there have been some CSOs seeking legitimacy, credibility and trust owing to operating in a conflict zone, economic collapse or political shifts.

The question of funding will remain a crucial issue for CSOs' operations and scope of work in Middle East countries in the post-pandemic era as a result of various political and economic conditions and shifts. The foreign donors' community has already reallocated its available resources to their local and domestic needs as the global market and business has been shrinking and witnessing very hard times. Therefore, CSOs have to explore and raise funding from local resources and recruit volunteers to continue their engagement, deliveries and services to their own people, target groups and beneficiaries.

Challenges to civil society organisations' public diplomacy 103

CSOs in stable and democratic societies such as Ireland, Wales and Scotland have adapted to the sudden and surprising changes owing to COVID-19 as they emerged. These shifts will be lessons to be learnt on how activists and leaders of CSOs in these societies worked differently, how we could predict a different future based on that learning, and how the significance and impact of the COVID-19 pandemic on the civil society sector are tackled. The civil society sectors of these countries have faced similar circumstances and challenges while meeting the demands of their vulnerable communities. Some CSOs' leaders, however, show exceptional and phenomenal skills and innovative approaches to keep their organisations alive and save the jobs of their staff while engaging with their volunteers, target groups, board members and funders online. The governments of these countries have already assisted the sector in facing the existential threat by launching schemes and funds to support staff salaries and programmes.

References

Aragonès, E. and Sánchez-Pagés, S. (2009), 'A theory of participatory democracy based on the real case of Porto Alegre', European Economic Review 53 (1) (2009), 56–72.

Bherer, L., Dufour, P. and Montambeault, F. (2016), 'The participatory democracy turn: an introduction', Journal of Civil Society 12 (3), 225–230.

Busan Global Partnership Forum for Effective Development Cooperation. (29 November-1 December 2011), available at: https://www.oecd.org/dac/effectiveness/49650173.pdf.

Carmody, P., McCann, G., Colleran, C. and O'Halloran, C. (2020) COVID-19 in the global south: Impacts and responses. UK: Bristol University Press.

CIVICUS. (2020) State of Civil Society Report 2020, The year in review. Johannesburg

CIVICUS. (2019) State of civil society report 2019 – The year in review. Johannesburg.

De Harder, C. (2020) 'A Polarised Nation during a Global Pandemic: the Libyan Predicament,' Civil society platform for peacebuilding and statebuilding.

Dionigi, F., (2016) The Syrian refugee crisis in Lebanon: state fragility and social resilience (LSE Middle East Centre paper series 15). London. available at: http://eprints.lse.ac.uk/65565/.

Elfeituri, N. (2020) 'Why Civil Society is Libya's Best Defense Against the COVID-19 Pandemic', Middle East Report Online.

Fathi Tomi (2017) Interviewed. Libyan Activist. Dublin. (22 August 2017).

Gerring, J. (2011) 'The case study: What it is and what it does' in Robert E. Goodin (ed.), The Oxford Handbook of Political Science (Oxford, 2011), 2–38

Hilmer, J. (2010) 'The State of Participatory Democratic Theory', New Political Science, 32 (1), 43–63.

Human Rights Watch. (13 July 2020) 'Lebanon: New Coalition to Defend Free Speech', available at: https://www.hrw.org/news/2020/07/13/lebanon-new-coalition-defend-free-speech.

104 *Ibrahim Natil*

Hulme, D. and Horner, R. (2020), 'After the immediate coronavirus crisis: 3 scenarios for global development', Global policy.

Jalbout, M. (2020) IFI Op-ed #21: Why MENA needs to change the way It supports civil Society? AUB Issam Fares Institute.

Khalfallah, A. (2020) 'Lebanon: Civil society in the face of crisis', available at: https://atalayar.com/en/blog/lebanon-civil-society-face-crisis.

Khalifa, A. (2020) Conflict and coronavirus – Libyan women pay the higher price. Qantara.de.

Lewis, E. (2020) 'Coronavirus: Domestic violence grows under Lebanon's lockdown', available at: https://english.alarabiya.net/features/2020/04/13/Coronavirus-Domestic-violence-grows-under-Lebanon-s-lockdown.

McCloskey, S. (2020) The Impact of the War in Syria on Palestinian Refugees in Lebanon and Syria. Belfast. UK

Mullard, S and Aarvik, P. (2020) Supporting civil society during the Covid-19 pandemic. Bergen.

Natil, I. (2014) 'A shifting political landscape: NGOs' civic activism and response in the Gaza Strip, 1967–2014', Journal of Peacebuilding & Development, 9 (3) (2014), 82–87.

Natil, I. (2019) 'The power of civil society: young leaders' engagement in nonviolent actions in Palestine', in Ibrahim Natil, Chiara Pieroban and Lilian Tauber (eds.), The Power of Civil Society in the Middle East and North Africa: Peacebuilding, Change and Development (Oxford and New York).

Natil, I. (2020) 'Women's community peacebuilding in the occupied Palestinian territories (OPT)', in Oliver Richmond and Gazim Visoka (eds.), The Palgrave encyclopedia of peace and conflict studies (Cham).

Natil, I. (2020) 'Introducing barriers to effective civil society organisations' in Ibrahim Natil, Vanessa Malila and Youcef Sai (eds.), Barriers to effective civil society organisations: Political, social and financial shifts. Oxford and New York: Routledge.

OECD. (2011) How DAC members work with civil society organisations: An overview (Paris, 2011).

Paffenholz, T. (2010) Civil society & peacebuilding: A critical assessment. Boulder.

Paffenholz, T. and Spurk, C. (2010) 'A comprehensive analytical framework,' in Thania Paffenholz (ed.), Civil Society & Peacebuilding: A Critical Assessment. Boulder.

Peters, K. and El Taraboulsi-McCarthy, S. (2020) Dealing with COVID-19 in conflict zones needs a different approach. Thomson Reuters Foundation.

Pulla, V., Jaysawal, N. and Saha, S. (2019) 'Challenges and dilemmas of civil society movements in India,' Asian social work and policy review 13, 169–178.

Sigman, R. and Lindberg, S. (2019) 'Democracy for all: conceptualizing and measuring egalitarian democracy', Political science research and methods 7 (3), 595–612.

United Nations Development Programme (UNDP) (2019) COVID-19 and human development assessing the crisis, envisioning the recovery. New York.

United Nations Office for the Coordination of Humanitarian Affairs (OCHA) (2020) 'How COVID-19 measures affect women, girls, men and boys differently', Reliefweb online.

Challenges to civil society organisations' public diplomacy 105

UNICEF. (7 July 2020) 'Institutions from UN Lebanon, the Lebanese government and the civil society urge all individuals and sectors to strengthen the preventive measures against COVID-19', available at: https://www.unicef.org/lebanon/press-releases/institutions-un-lebanon-lebanese-government-and-civil-society-urge-all-individuals.

Weeden, L. (2015) 'Abandoning 'legitimacy': reflections on Syria and Yemen', in M. Hudson (ed.), The Crisis of the Arab State – Study Group Report. Cambridge.

Wiggers, R. (2016) 'Action for children: A model for stimulating local fundraising in low and middle-income countries', Development in practice 26 (5) (2016), 619–628.

World Health Organization (2020) Listings of WHO's response to COVID-19. Geneva.

Yahya, M. (2020) 'Lebanon is struggling against simultaneous shocks, and the country is in urgent need of a new social contract', 31 January 2020, available at: https://carnegie-mec.org/diwan/region/1406?lang=en&pageOn=4.

Youngs, R. and Panchulidze, E. (2020) 'Global Democracy & COVID-19: Upgrading International Support', European endowment for democracy.

9 Concluding thoughts

New directions for civil society organisations' public diplomacy

Ibrahim Natil

This book distinguishes itself as a new approach to civil society in the global context, by focusing on public diplomacy and civil society organisations. Scholars, for example, (Cameroon, Egypt, Poland, Ireland, Palestine and Jordan) will reflect on CSOs in development, politics and business and their impact on community development initiatives and local change process. Their debate and argument supported by field work, participatory observation, interviews and making references to the existing literature. The main contributions of the book are to undertake new research, particularly around informed practice on the ground, and to present recommendations to policymakers and donors on better ways of providing space for CSO contributions on specific policy issues. We hope this book would provide insights and stimulate others to conduct further work in this growing area of research. It concludes with some implications and offers some direction for future research in the field of CSOs' public diplomacy campaigns and their impact on sustainable business and development in non-western contexts.

The book, however, is addressed to undergraduates, postgraduates, scholars and professionals. It covers mostly intermediate and advanced levels in the academic sphere, but is also useful to professionals working in development and business. The book is also of interest to the general public and contributes to the field of development, business, politics and international relations, conflict resolution and peacebuilding, civil society and foreign aid. This new approach is particularly strong because it is based not only on empirical discussions of individual countries, but also on a firm theoretical framework of the discussion of CSOs leadership and development issues. In this way, our volume significantly contributes to theoretical discussions of the complexities of civil society organisations' engagement in public diplomacy activities in responding to various changes and shifts at political, social, domestic, national and global levels.

Public diplomacy scope of work is not restricted to the state's functions or foreign policy staff and diplomates abroad. No state actors have

DOI: 10.4324/9781003441465-9

Concluding thoughts 107

become significant players or influential contributors at diplomatic level, owing to the complexities of issues and level of interactions among states, non-states as international and civil society organisations and citizens. The complexities of interactions among the various nations of the globe, owing to available tools of technology and free access to social media networks that encourage individuals, companies, schools, clubs, etc to get engaged, for example, in public diplomacy activities. The revolution of digital information technology has contributed to development of public diplomacy concept and practice. This can be understood as a new diplomacy dynamics and mechanism when engage with locals and grassroots via social networks to disseminate information to brand a certain country's identity or influence public opinions.

Non-state actors engage and practice public diplomacy to influence national or and foreign public opinions too. Influencing publics abroad is not only the job of the states, but also the non-state actors as CSOs do. CSOs have become functional across the board and share the same values, concerns, interests, problems, common grounds and issues. CSOs work easily with their partner CSOs within certain networks across borders and at the global level to advocate for their common values and issues. In other words, their issues of interest are common values with many diplomatic missions, democratic states or even non-democratic states. CSOs might find sponsors as companies and diplomatic missions to tackle certain issues to achieve their common goals. These common values are a part and parcel of public diplomacy campaigns for both states, donors or diplomatic missions, owing to mutual interests and engaging with foreign citizens or public opinions abroad.

Not the question if the CSOs' leadership, staff, volunteer at the local or and national level are aware of engaging in public diplomacy activities or if they understand what public diplomacy in a technical terms. In other words, local CSOs have no plan to launch or react to diplomatic diplomacy activities; however, they design activities that meet the standards and requirements of donors to publicise financial support of the sponsor. Of course, they are aware why the embassy or diplomatic mission requires CSOs to make their logos visible or to publicise the financial support throughout the community by using new social media networks or traditional media.

However, there are many CSOs, which are capable of engaging at the global level via international platforms such as UN or EU or other forums to promote or brand their issue or cause. These CSOs have massive networks in various fields from human rights to peacebuilding, democracy, women and gender etc. These platforms have massive access to share information, expertise, ideas and common issues. This assists CSOs to get involved in complicated environments of communications, interactions and exchange, where multiple levels of professional staff

108 *Ibrahim Natil*

from experts, activists, diplomats, scholars, academics, trainers engage in this process of formal or informal public diplomacy practice. Today, new public diplomacy includes a component or a mixtures of activities, approaches, philosophies, techniques, tools, tactics and strategies, which might involve "cultural, sport, human rights, development, education, art, etc." This mixture of activities is not overlapped; however, this will contribute to achieve the goals of the foreign policy in a third country. It depends on the objectives and priorities of foreign policy in the targeted countries, where the citizens' should be actively involved and participated via CSOs or other pattern of engagement.

Certain donors or diplomatic missions have specific clients/CSOs to finance at the long term or short term. In other words, donors and diplomatic missions also compete with each other as CSOs do. However, CSOs' civic engagement and public diplomacy actions at the global, national and even local level have been facing a shrinking space imposed by military attacks, violence and political restrictions on their human rights actions. The Israeli government, for example, has led systematic operations of smear, defamation, and defunding campaigns by Israeli and international lobby groups such as NGO Monitor and UK Lawyers for Israel at different levels against the Palestinian and international organisations supporting human rights activities. Israel has banned more than 400 local and international organisations as being "hostile" or "unlawful" since 1967. There are the recent military attacks on civil society organisations (CSOs) by the Israeli occupation forces, who raided the offices of six leading Palestinian civil society and human rights organisations in the occupied city of the West Bank, Ramallah. On August 18th they were outlawed by Israel as "terrorist" organisations in October 2021, and accused of having connections to the Popular Front for the Liberation of Palestine (PFLP).

These organisations including Addameer Prisoner Support and Human Rights Association, Al-Haq rights group, the Union of Palestinian Women Committees (UPWC), the Union of Agricultural Work Committees (UAWC), the Bisan Center for Research and Development, and the Palestine chapter of the Geneva-based Defence for Children International, have been operating for many years and were funded by international donors as European organisations in particular. They are a key pillar of the larger Palestinian civil society in delivering asocial and economic development services for Palestinians who live in the 1967-occupied territories.

These organisations regularly try people for work exercising basic civil rights and for criticising the Israeli occupation. The Israeli measures to tighten restrictions on civil society nearly a year after it labelled the organisations, which was widely condemned by the international community as "unjustified" and "baseless." In addition to this, European

Concluding thoughts 109

donor countries including Netherlands, Denmark, Norway and Switzerland have found no evidence to endorse the Israeli government's claims against the six organisations. The actions of closing offices or targeting human rights organisations may encourage not only more young scholars to research and learn in-depth about neo-colonisers' behaviours, attitudes but also attract more solidarity and support from various activists and institutions. Why did Israel not care about increasing the support and solidarity with the Palestinians globally?

These actions have increased these CSOs engagement in public diplomacy activities across the borders. The Israeli human rights organisation along with 46 other civil society organisations have stood in solidarity with their Palestinian colleagues facing the draconian measures of the Israeli regime. These organisations have also received regional and international support and solidarity after their offices were attacked, for example, a group of 15 Arab progressive parties from various countries, Algeria, Tunisia, Lebanon, Egypt, etc. These progressive parties called upon the progressive human rights bodies and anti-occupation forces around the world to organise the necessary events and activities to expose and defame the coercive policies. These measures of attacking civil and human rights organisations are a part of the comprehensive policy of eradicating the Palestinian existence in the occupied territories by killing their powerful and influential voices.

Public diplomacy campaigns run by local, Arab and international CSOs increased after the killing of Shireen Abu Akleh in Jenin on May 11, 2022. Killing a journalist who was an icon of public diplomacy for freedom of speech, marginalised people and women groups living under foreign occupation not only shocked the world, but also created a new space to expose and document the Israeli policies of human rights violations in an unprecedented scene. There were many local and international journalists in the occupied Palestinian territories. On May 15, 2021, Israel's air forces bombed and destroyed the offices in the multistorey building of 20 floors in Gaza City. The building housed well-known international media agencies as Reuters, Associated Press, and Al Jazeera network, which issued a statement. Israel clearly understands that the free journalists and reports expose its actions of human rights violations of killing, houses and farms destruction, lands confiscations, assassinations, arrest of minors, collective punishment against the Palestinian, which contradicts the international laws including the Geneva Convention.

In other words, journalists are real peaceful freedom fighters who inform the world about Israel's violation of human rights as did Shireen Abu Akleh, an icon of public diplomacy. Abu Akleh was an exceptional and distinguished international reporter who worked in a very complicated political and security environment, while covering various events in Palestine owing to the Israeli occupation. She stayed steadfast, brave

110 *Ibrahim Natil*

and professional ever since she began her job in 1996. As her colleague, Walid Al Omer, who worked closely together said:

> "She was an exceptional reporter, not only in Palestine, but also at the global level." She was a well-known reporter, professional and internationally respected who met the editorial policy of its employer "Al Jazeera Network."

Abu Akleh, however, introduced the Palestinian cause and narratives by covering the Israeli' violations since 1996. Abu Akleh inspired generations who dream to follow her legacy, mission, work, values, etc. She believed she was serving a "Cause" as a professional in accordance with international standards of journalism and reporting about events while working for a well-known network, "Al Jazeera." She quitted engineering studies, her parent's first choice, for journalism and media studies. Her desire and ambition was to be close to the people's issue, suffering, and to cover stories and communicate human issues to the world. Her desire was to get close to the voiceless, marginalised and vulnerable people who lived in a complicated environment, owing to the Israeli occupation policies in the Palestinian territories.

However, she also covered events that affected the Palestinians community in Israel and the international arena as in the USA. She was an exceptional woman and a figure of unity, resilience, and defiance who fought for her cause, society and humanity at large. In addition, she used to donate for Jerusalemites children, orphans and poor people who have suffered from Israeli systematic policies. She also used to join the Muslim prayers in the Alqsa mosque, despite the fact she was a Christian. There were many people lived in her city, Jerusalem and across the Palestinian communities, who did not know her faith. Abu Akleh united Palestinian faiths who prayed together at her funeral. It was phenomenal that this had never happened before. Both faiths marched and prayed together for a woman in Palestine. All churches from all faiths united together and paid tribute to Abu Akleh who captured the minds and the hearts of all Palestinians. There have been generations who grew up with Shireen's distinguished voice. They believed that she was their voice and represented their "Cause". In other words, she was the voice of voiceless people. Anger, sorrow and sadness shocked them when they learned she was shot by the Israeli occupying forces, which was infiltrating into the city of Jenin in the North of West Bank.

The killing of Shireen shocked the Palestinian society, and various political and social spectrum and movements put aside their differences and problems to respond together to the legacy of Shireen. CSOs and local groups activated campaigns to condemn the killing of Abu Akleh Shireen and united the world in denying Israel's deliberate attack on her

Concluding thoughts 111

despite the fact she was known as a journalist, and wore a protective vest that is labelled "PRESS" on both the front and back. The world and free press also covered the scenes at her funeral, where the Israeli soldiers prevented her mourners from walking on foot to the cemetery. The horrible attack shocked not only the Palestinian but also the free people from different spectrums who called for an independent International commission of enquiry; however, some western press such as the New York Times discriminated against and were biased against Shireen by describing her "death" while reporting about the killing of an American journalist by Russians. However, Shireen was an American citizen who was brought up in Palestine. The double standard policy of coverage by western media has been clearly strange when it comes to Palestine cause. CNN, however, supported by footage by CNN, corroborated by testimony from eight eyewitnesses, indicated that Israeli forces intentionally aimed at Abu Akleh.

There have been a number of local and international organisations commemorating her legacy by launching programmes as Berizt University has done. The municipality of Birah in the West Bank, named a road in her name. A number of Abu Akleh's colleagues at various locations around the world, marched to protest Israel's actions. Anger and sorrow have increased after watching the Israeli forces attacking her funeral while men from both faiths carried her coffin. In honour of her, the Arab League adopts May 11 of every year as a day of media solidarity with the Palestinian media, the day on which journalist, Abu Akleh was killed. Despite the strong belief and the evidence from various sources indicating that she was killed by the Israeli forces, Israel denies criminalising their soldiers as mentioned in their own investigation that there is a "high possibility" that one of its soldiers killed Abu Akleh. Her family, however, continues to fight for justice via all possible avenues. Israel is not worried about accountability before the international community and it believes it is protected and above international law. Israel targets journalists, reporters, and human rights in a systematic policy to frighten and terrify them to hide the expanding Israeli apartheid system every day in Palestine.

In spite of massive challenges facing CSOs at different levels, they are able to accommodate and adopt new tactics, techniques, strategies, activities and tools of public diplomacy to respond to social, political, economic and health including climate changes. There have been a number of local and global civil society organisations that address climate changes issues. The current crises of environment and development have profoundly shaken the ways researchers and practitioners work in/ with non-governmental organisations (NGOs) /civil society organisation (CSOs) across the world. This future research will aim to provide a platform for sharing practitioners' and researchers' experiences and

112 *Ibrahim Natil*

reflections on crises of environment and development through the lens of the Anthropocene. This will bring together some case studies from various places around the world to highlight the challenges and opportunities for engaging researchers, policymakers and practitioners and CSOs/NGOs' activists to discuss a number of issues, for example, resilience in theory of change, resilience in challenging climate changes, the role of NGOs in challenging the current crisis as the impact of COVID-19. What does the Anthropocene mean for established NGOs and unsettled civil society organisations (CSOs)? To what extent do NGOs/CSOs challenge the current global crisis (climate changes, the impact COVID-19), which has profoundly shaken the ways researchers and practitioners work in/with NGOs and (CSOs), in the global south and the global north. Virtually all NGOs have been affected by the COVID-19 pandemic and climate changes, the impact has been different in each country, according to its specific geopolitical position, the urban/rural settings, the resources available and governments' responses.

Index

business 6, 9, 10, 19, 26, 106

campaigns 1, 2, 6, 11, 13, 41, 66, 78, 106
change 1, 2, 43, 51, 71, 75
civil society 1, 2, 3, 5, 7, 9, 10, 11, 26, 29, 30, 32, 34, 37, 44, 50, 57, 62, 67, 74, 106, 108–112
civil society organisations (CSOs) 1, 5, 10, 29, 32, 41, 74, 69, 74, 76, 106, 107, 108
communications 1, 2, 4, 10, 12, 69, 107
Covid-19 3, 6, 7, 16, 67, 68, 112
CSOs 1, 2, 3, 4, 5, 6, 7, 8, 9, 10, 11, 12, 13, 14, 16, 17–29, 30, 31, 32, 33–112
cultural 1, 75, 108
culture 1, 3, 5, 6, 7, 10

development 1, 2, 3, 4, 7, 8, 9, 10, 11, 30, 33, 41, 43, 44, 45, 47, 50, 61, 77, 106, 108
digital 1, 4, 16, 107
diplomatic missions 1, 2, 3, 5, 13, 14, 25, 26, 30, 108
donors 1, 2, 3, 7, 12, 13, 17, 64, 78, 79, 107, 108

engagement 1–2, 3, 4, 7, 9, 10, 11, 12, 15, 17, 19, 33, 36, 58, 62, 66, 68, 69, 70, 74, 85, 108

Global South 4, 43, 112
grassroots 1, 4, 11, 12, 16, 107

human rights 2, 3, 13, 12, 14, 15, 49, 64, 71, 75, 107, 108, 109

leaders 6, 7, 10, 11, 12, 31, 32

media 9, 11, 14, 13, 15, 16, 32, 107, 110

NGOs 2, 4, 10, 30, 31, 32, 33, 34, 35, 36, 83, 84, 85, 111, 108, 112

operations 1, 4, 7, 16, 67, 69
organisations 1, 2, 3, 4, 5, 6, 7, 10, 12, 50, 109, 111

peacebuilding 3, 7, 10, 12, 107
platforms 1, 16, 74, 107
political 1, 3, 5, 6, 7, 19, 37, 45, 48, 49, 56, 59, 61, 65, 67, 69, 70, 74, 76, 78, 85, 106, 109, 111
public diplomacy 1, 2, 3, 4, 5, 6, 7, 9, 10, 11, 12, 17, 29, 30, 31, 33, 36, 37, 55, 74, 106–112

scholarship 2, 3, 48
soft power 9, 11, 15, 30, 43